MW00422658

U.S. Fucking History

The Textbook that Won't Put You to Sleep

By Author S. Names

Copyright© 2018

All Rights Reserved

ISBN: 978-1-718-1290-61

To Reif & The Reader

Just Kidding Fuck the Reader lol

Table of Contents

Pre-1700s: We Live in a Society

(1500s-1611) THE ENGLISH FUCKING UP: THE STORY OF AMERICA

WALTER RALEIGH: NEW IN TOWN

Three centuries before the English would fuck up staying in North America (1776, 1812, etc.), they'd fuck up actually entering North America in the first place. While much of Europe (most notably the Spanish) had successfully established colonies by the late 1500s, England was just starting out. Sir Walter Raleigh attempted first to establish English presence in Roanoke Island, North Carolina in 1584. Raleigh's colony went to shit almost immediately, so he tried again in 1585, which went to shit, and finally he tried once more in 1587. This colony was actually never heard from again. All of its inhabitants vanished, and people are still wondering what went wrong. The most likely answer? It went to shit.

TL;DR England was late to the game colonizing the New World. They tried in the late 1500s and it didn't work.

WHY JAMESTOWN?

England had been monumentally fucked in the New World so far, but by the early 1600s, they were so incredibly fucked domestically that they were willing to try colonization again. In 1607, about a hundred settlers landed in Jamestown, Virginia to create the first permanent colony of England (which, in case you were wondering, nearly went to shit).

What drove England to try again? A combination of things. Urbanization ran wild as England's population boomed. Cities became overcrowded and wages were suffering as a result. Internationally, previous fuck-uppery had left England far behind the competition, and the likelihood of Spain controlling the majority of the New World threatened England's status. Finally, as Protestantism grew in England, the more extreme Puritans (Calvinists) saw the New World as a potential place to grow their own ideology. Within the next decades, as the Church shifted back towards Catholic tradition under Stuart rule, this became more of a push to avoid persecution than an aggressive move by the Puritans. Long story short, all kinds of people immigrated to America if only to get the fuck out of England.

TL;DR In a conceited effort to prove its dick was bigger than Spain's, find more room for all it's new people, and find new room for its more Puritan people, England tried to colonize North America again in Jamestown.

JAMESTOWN ORIGINS: THEY SUCKED

In May of 1607, The Jamestown Colony (chartered by—surprise—King James I) was settled by just over a hundred British merchants. They were looking for precious metals, trade opportunities, and basically what all merchants are always looking for: Money.

Jamestown's colonizers—the Virginia Company—were funded by a joint stock company, which is basically the old version of crowdsourcing. Like all crowdsourcing ventures, however, the people investing their money got bored of the project once it wasn't cool anymore, and funding was low from the beginning. This especially sucked for Jamestown because they took a long time to get on their feet, and much of that time was spent being uncool.

Why did Jamestown struggle so much to become semi-independent? A number of things got in the way. Jamestown at the time had an awful climate for guests, and Virginia Co. arrived in the middle of a drought. This problem expanded into a spread of disease as the new colonists drank the same river water they washed clothes in. Jamestown was awful for guests, but it was especially awful for the lazy-fuck guests. Just like their investors, colonists were very into "getting rich" and "quick," but didn't want to do the dirty labor that came with those goals. Afterall, they had just gotten off the ship they'd been on for the last 144 days.

Who could blame them? Everyone. Nine out of ten of the first group of colonists died from the bad luck and bad work ethic of the new immigrants.

On the bright side, however, there was finally a government for those that lived. By 1619, the House of Burgesses was created to give the people of Jamestown representation in their local government. Elections were held democratically in Massachusetts as well, but in both colonies democracy still existed only to a degree.

TL;DR Merchants and other Brits settled Jamestown in 1607, which was, weather- wise, really bad timing. A lot of them died because they were lazy, underfunded, and generally covered in dirt. They got to have some representation in government though which was nice, but not solving any of their problems.

JAMESTOWN GETS DESPERATE: THEN MEAN

Things in Jamestown got so bad that the British imperialists had to go against all their principles and do the unthinkable: befriend to the native people.

Powhatan, leader of the Powhatan Confederacy of the local Native-American tribes, took a chance on the merchants in a display of friendship and dumbassery. He traded much needed food to the immigrants in exchange for weapons and artisan goods, hoping to use the former to stabilize his Confederacy. This relationship deteriorated to a brooding peace, caused by British misunderstanding of native culture and governmental style, coupled with the fact that they didn't really give a shit, especially when it came to the natives' belief in communal land ownership. Looking forward, British goals became more about stealing land than trading goods. They'd continue fighting with the Powhatan throughout the rest of the century.

TL;DR English colonists befriended and traded with the locals out of desperation. They then proceeded to take advantage of and kill the natives for the rest of the century.

(1611-1660) SMOKING IS COOL! TOBACCO, RELIGION, AND OTHER THINGS

DRUGS: THEY SAVED THE WORLD (kinda)

What ended up being the reason for the colonists not screwing up again? Well, it was everyone's favorite new addiction: tobacco. Who would've guessed it? It took the merchant colonists until 1611 to find the crop they needed to rake in the easy money they'd been looking for since they landed. They started selling this shit like there was no tomorrow, (probably because for 90% of them there had been no tomorrow until now) and so much so that tobacco itself became like a currency. Because of this, the colony kept growing into an significant settlement that Britain could ACTUALLY be proud of (and subsequently tax the shit out of without representation). They needed more land for the tobacco, too, because early growing practices wore out soil quickly. As the colony expanded economically, it also had to expand just as much geographically.

TL;DR Tobacco became a cash crop. The land in Jamestown happened to be perfect for growing it, so naturally the colonists overused that land until they had to move on and take more of other people's land. This is called expansion.

BRITISH EXPANSION (AND INTERFERENCE) CAUSES CONFLICT: SHOCKER

This expansion typically involved pissing off local natives, notably Powhatan's successor, whose name is too long for anybody to put on a standardized test or for you to remember anyway. The Native-American Confederacy responded by attacking a bunch of colonists up and down the James River in March of 1622. This killed about a quarter of the colonists, and also dismantled, finally, the Virginia Company, which wasn't even making money anymore. The colony once possessed by a joint stock venture became a Royal Colony. It didn't help the colonists' case that their dumbass founders had started their settlement by trading weapons to the Confederacy, and

---

continued it by repeatedly abusing their trust. The colonists fought back nonetheless with reinforcements, and forced the natives to sign a treaty in April of 1644, which declared them to be legally "lesser" than the English (foreshadowing???).

As the Native-Americans were giving up power to the colonists, the crown was focused on taking power from the colonists. Following the 1622 attacks and the Virginia Company's transition to a royal colony, James I attempted to dismantle the colonists' House of Burgesses —their first taste at independent government. Understandably, the colonists were fuckin' angry about that, so the British ruler had to give up (foreshadowing pt. 2).

Back in England, the imperialists were still hungry for more imperialism, so in 1634, King Charles I gave a guy named George Calvert some land on the Chesapeake to use as personal property. This became Maryland. Calvert wanted to be a nice guy, so he gave religious freedom to Roman Catholics. He obviously made a good impression, because his son, Cecil Calvert, turned Maryland into the first colony to give religious freedom to all people. Except anyone who wasn't a Christian (but it's a start).

Because the British like to steal things from people, and in this case, themselves, Maryland was basically a carbon-copy of Virginia. Aside from religion, both colonies were made up of ex-Englishmen, relied heavily on tobacco as a cash crop, and used rivers to transport their shit.

The Massachusetts Bay Colony was also founded in this time, as John Winthrop led a group of disenfranchised English Puritans on a search for religious freedom in 1630. Thousands more followed suit, triggering "the Great Migration" and setting a precedent for mass immigration to the colonies.

TL;DR As the British expanded into new territories, they started a tradition of killing the Native resistance in their way. Ownership of the colony was transferred from the Virginia Company to the Crown, which pushed expansion further and spurred the beginnings of conflict between the governors and the governed.

OTHER PEOPLE ARE GETTING INVOLVED

While the English were taking more of New England, the Spanish and French were conquering land in other parts of America.

The Spaniards were having a hard time with their efforts to wrap their imperial dicks around the corners of America. From the onset of Spanish expansion into the New World in the mid-1500s, they struggled to invade Florida multiple times before the Native-Americans gave up. This wasn't a huge loss for the natives because all in all, its just Florida. The Spanish didn't stop there, however, and spent the entire 1600s trying to colonize New Mexico. They were successful at first, and then for some godforsaken reason (pun intended) decided to try and force all the Native-Americans in the area to become Christians, which got the Spanish kicked out and wasted a century of work.

After they were kicked out of New Mexico, they resettled in Texas, a location to be

revisited during the Mexican-American War. The Spaniards, ignoring how the natives felt,

still claimed to own pretty much all of the New World, and split this claim with Portugal, taking everything east of Brazil and leaving Portugal to take...Brazil. They weren't the only ones trying to stake a claim to the New World though, and France set out to prove that. The French sent explorers Giovanni da Verrazzano and Jacques Cartier to investigate the east coast in the early 1500s, and eventually settled into a life of fur trading in the center of North America, with a base camp in Quebec, at the head of the St. Lawrence river, and a large presence in modern day Canada. The French had wars and shit to deal with at home, so they took a long time to settle in to the New World, and were quick to sell their stakes in the Jefferson

Purchase of 1803. The Dutch also got a foot in the door, naming and exploring the Hudson river, as well as founding the colony of New York, but that's not really important to know unless you play trivia games (nerd).

TL;DR The Spaniards and French both made major land claims in the New World, and the Dutch stopped by for a bit as well. Everyone struggled to hold onto their land though, the Spaniards because they got a little to into Catholicism, and the French because they got a little to into Europe.

AMERICANS ARE "WELCOMING" TO "IMMIGRANTS"

As tobacco was growing, both in farms and as an economic source for the colonies, the sheer amount of people moving in to work on tobacco farms became a problem. Again, English people liked ruling over shit, and money, so they chose to solve this problem by making other people work for them. So began the headright system and, therefore, indentured servitude.

Basically, the headright system was new legislation stating that any immigrants (only ones who paid for the boat ride, no stowaways) could get 50 acres of land to work on. A lot of Englishmen who had money to develop that land heard about this, and it encouraged them to take the risk and come on over. The system also really benefited people who were already here, because it gave them some new land to work on and new labor to work it with.

Just like the colonists first who first arrived years earlier, these wealthy, new, primarily English immigrants were lazy and looking to get rich quick. They started paying for other people's passages to the New World in exchange for their "indentured servitude," a contract that bound them to work for their sponsor for a certain number of years as repayment. Should almost sound familiar. The new planters would essentially get temporary but nearly free labor, and the laborers would get their freedom (and their own land) after a few years of work.

While great in theory, the workers ended up getting pretty much, well, fucked over by this deal. They never got the freedom they worked for if they died before they were done working, and awful conditions led to this often. The system was visibly imperfect, but as long as the courts were giving free shit away, people would be lined up to get their hands on it, so the tobacco boom still provided some real opportunities...until it didn't. In 1670, as land became more and more scarce and prices fell, shit hit the fan in Maryland when the colonial government dropped the requirement that ex-indentured servants be granted land in 1681. As people began to see that all their work was for nothing, they lost trust in the colonial economy, and the sharp decline in growth that followed showed that this legislative turning point would be the end of the first American economic boom.

TL;DR Rich English people got lazy and started paying for other people to do work in exchange for a boat ride to America. The tobacco boom attracted many new immigrants at first, but people in power started getting stingier and giving out less stuff, closing the first economic boom of the New World off in the 1670s.

ENGLAND WANTS MORE SHIT

England starts expanding even more, with two main groups starting the settlements in the North (at least north of Virginia).

The separatists (or Pilgrims), well, separated from the Anglican Church because they were worried about corruption.

The Congregationalists (or Puritans) were the absolutely fucking psychotic ones who wanted to purify the Anglican Church even more, thinking it was too Catholic. They were also kinda known as Calvinists.

After a while, more and more people came, but they weren't all Pilgrims or Puritans. Lots of people came for various money-related reasons. However, the religious ideals of the original founders stuck around for quite a long time.

TL;DR Even more people join the adolescent, healthy colonies because they didn't like how religion has been working in England.

THE PILGRIMS AND THEIR SHIT

English folks started their colonization of New England (because of course they'd name it after themselves) with a pilgrim congregation who got permission from the Virginia Company to move out north. They left aboard the Mayflower in September of 1620. If you didn't know the boat was called the Mayflower, then maybe this shouldn't be the first history book you're reading. The leaders had to make sure they were still leaders by the time they landed, so they put together the Mayflower Compact. Basically, it established this half assed system of government called a "civil body politic," which was a declaration that essentially said "we're all just gonna pitch and and make some laws and they will be good laws because we said so." They were also moderately extremist, so they had to specify that this would be an egalitarian colony (for church people only) and that they would be drawn together by communalism. Not to be confused with communism.

Either way, the Pilgrims landed on November 21, 1620. They named their town after what they ate on the ship, Plymouth. Creative. They had a shit time at the beginning because they, like many colonists, didn't know what the fuck, or rather, *where the fuck,* they were dealing with, especially when it came to the climate. Luckily, a local Native tribe had also lost a bunch of people to a recent disease, and decided they wanted to stick with the English for some god-forsaken reason. They flourished for a bit, but then...

TL;DR Some people came to America on the Mayflower, north of Jamestown and stuff, and created basic legal systems to help get society off the ground. They were failing, but got some help from Natives around the area.

THE PURITANS AND THEIR SHIT

The Pilgrims started to struggle a bit, as most dumbass English colonies do, and then another group came and started their own settlement. They were, obviously, the Puritans. They eventually absorbed Plymouth into Puritan territory in 1691. At the top of their food chain were Congregationalists, the psychotic ones we talked about earlier. They'd been kicked out of England by Charles I (probably for good reason), who started to get rid of their practices.

In 1629, the weirdass Congregationalists somehow got an actual charter and formed the Massachusetts Bay Company. A lot of the Puritans in England saw this as their golden ticket out of a continually worse situation in their homeland. They still wanted to remake the church, though, so some stayed with their losing battle and some immigrated to the new frontier.

A lot of merchants who came over to the colonies decided that they'd probably have to actually settle down and make their HQ in America. John Winthrop was elected governor of a large new group of immigrants, (and what would soon become the Massachusetts Bay Colony) and the gang set sail in October of 1629. Much to everyone's dismay, they landed in 1630. Like most absolute fucking sociopaths, Johnny boy decided to make a speech while aboard their ship, the Arbella. He used a sermon to explain his views for the new colony, and it was called "The Model of Christian Charity". He wanted to put a stress on community, a covenant with God, and looked to making a sort of utopian "City on a Hill" (yep, that's Boston). It took a while for actual institutions to make his speech come true, one which was the General Court, originally governed for the company. It was soon changed into a two- house colonial legislature, and is one of the earliest examples of colonial attempts at self government.

TL;DR This religious guy, John Winthrop, brought a whole new wave of money- hungry English people with him to found the Massachusetts Bay Colony. They even tried to make some self government too. Adorable.

NEW ENGLAND COLONIES ARE GETTING BIGGER. SHIT PUT IT BACK

There were three main types of towns that developed amongst the colonies: agricultural towns that worshiped Winthrop, seaports/merchant towns that worshipped money, and more commercialized agricultural towns that had a healthy enough balance.

The colonies spread not just in economic purpose, but geographically too. Connecticut, New Haven, and New Hampshire were founded in 1636, 1638, and 1638 respectively, and the rapid expansionism that comes with forming new colonies led to some hissy-fits between the natives and the colonists. For example, the colonists who founded Connecticut with Thomas Hooker (not a prostitute) ran into the Pequot tribe. These natives were much fucking smarter than the colonists, and knew that the English arrival threatened the Pequots status as middlemen between other Native-American groups and the colonists...

A war happened, triggered by the death of two English traders (ironically, this was not even caused by Pequots). The English overreacted and raided a Pequot village in response. The Natives understandably fought back in April of 1637, but then the English went way over the fucking top again and burned the main Pequot village, essentially destroying them forever.

Probably out of fear, the Natives allowed the colonists to expand as much as they liked into their land, and the both pretty much left each other alone. John Eliot was the only English dumbass who didn't learn his lesson, and tried to convert some natives to Christianity, but of course he failed horribly because he wanted them to totally reject every single goddamned thing they'd ever known...a pretty tough thing to sell when you meet all your customers by wandering around the woods with a bible.

TL;DR New England gets bigger and needs more Native land to expand. The Connecticut people and Tommy Hooker get into a war with the Pequots, burn their shit, then the Natives back off.

PEOPLE ARE DIFFERENT IN DIFFERENT PLACES. WHO KNEW?

Life and society evolved differently for the New England fuckheads than it did for the Chesapeake shitheads. Culture, values, climate— it was all different.

• Religious importance - Chesapeake people didn't really give a flying shit about religion until the 1690s, when the Church of England got its hands dirty in Virginia. However, they cared a lot about Christianity in New England. The Northeast had super strict moral codes, and anyone who disagreed with them could just get fuckin' exiled. Some famous people who did were Roger Williams, who founded Providence, Rhode Island, and Anne Hutchinson, who joined him. (A woman helping found a state! That's about as rare in America as good cholesterol.)

• Land distribution - In the Chesapeake colonies, land was distributed however people wanted to. They didn't give a shit. But in New England, a few people would apply together for grants of land, then plan a village so each person would get a piece of the pie.

• Towns and villages - The Chesapeake had mostly larger plantations, while New England was pretty much all small towns.

• Familial stuffs - They struggled a lot in the Chesapeake. There was an overwhelming dominance of males, higher death rates, and lots of indentured servitude. This led to smaller families which died earlier. In New England, though, people moved in families, making a male:female ratio that was much more even. This led to larger families which lived longer. It was much healthier and parents had some impact on their children's lives. And there were actual grandparents!

TL;DR Chesapeake people were tobacco farmers and New England people were religious fanatics who were a little more organized with land. Disclaimer: Some of the New England colonies were the least crazy about religion...but that was because their founders got kicked out of the other colonies by the religious fanatics there.

(1660-1700) RAPID COLONIAL EXPANSION: BECAUSE AMERICA IS DEFINITELY A GROWER

SOCIETY IN AMERICA BECOMES A THING

The English Parliament, led by Oliver Cromwell, rebelled against Charles I in 1642. They won four years later, and big shot Crommie led England until 1660. He was fucked up in a lot of ways, so the English wanted to put the monarchy back in place. They decided on Charles II. Very original.   This turmoil brought a lot of change to the colonies. Puritans under Crommie had controlled the government from the war until the restoration of the crown, so their migration to the colonies slowed down a lot. Also, post-1660, there were six new colonies formed. Now they were proprietorships!

- New York - Was originally a Dutch colony, but Charlie #2 gave it to his brother James, who was the Duke of York. They both decided to pretend that Dutch presence in the area didn't exist. They were basically right, as when James mustered an invasion fleet to settle the problem, the Dutch surrendered without almost any resistance, giving up control completely in 1674. NY also fostered religious tolerance, a big step from some of the weirdasses in New England.

- New Jersey - In 1664, James of New York lowkey fucked up by giving away a huge chunk of fantastic farming land to his friends Sir George Carteret and John Lord Berkeley, who used it to found NJ, a new, rapidly growing colony with some religious tolerance, self government, and land grants that attracted colonists in droves. It ended up in the hands of Quakers a couple decades later.

- Pennsylvania - Speaking of Quakers, William Penn opened Pennsylvania in 1681 as a triumph of religious freedom, tolerating almost everyone, even many Native-American immigrants.

- Carolina - The Carolina colony was a fertile farming base that was home to many immigrants. Founded in 1663 and organized by John Locke, it was a kinda feudal government that ended up falling apart into separate colonies in the early 1700s. The colony of North Carolina was better suited for crops like tobacco, while the South was lower swampier — best used for rice and indigo.

TL;DR The new colonies under Restoration-Age England (post-1660) were proprietorships that were for the most part pretty appealing to new colonists. To get to that point it took a lot of political fighting in England, but the colonists didn't really give a shit as long as they didn't have to do anything.

THE LATE SEVENTEENTH CENTURY

Just so you know, seventeenth century means 1600s. Now that that's out of the way, here's what happened. All the European colonies got into some shit with Native-Americans due to expansionism. The French, still on the fur trade grind, were attacking Iroquois villages to expand in the south and west (which ended in 1701 with a neutrality treaty). Spain on the other hand was going east and north, fucking up the Pueblo tribes along the way and trying to decimate their religion and culture. Not cool Spain. They struggled with Native-American resistance until the 1690s. In the English colonies, all the dumbass fighting came from land conflicts, particularly that the English people wanted to steal land from the Native-American people, which inevitably causes some sort of conflict. These skirmishes exploded into King Philip's war, which King Philip of the Pokanoket tribe kicked off by attacking English settlements in 1675. Even Plymouth and Providence were hit. Within a year the English had won, marking victory with King Philip's death, but their population was devastated nonetheless, and their economy unforgettably scarred.

Angry colonists in Virginia, however, were directly causing their own trouble for a change (as opposed to the more popular indirect method of consistently pissing off everyone else in the area until they had to fight back). They saw their Governor, William Berkeley, refusing to attack Native-Americans to give the colonists more land—he had lucrative trade deals with them that he sure as hell wasn't trying to fuck up—and gathered behind farmer Nathaniel Bacon, who led the charge to hold members of the House of Burgesses hostage until they agreed to attack the natives. By 1680, Bacon's forces had become engaged in battle with both their own government and Native-Americans, even burning Jamestown to the ground. As Bacon succeeded (and then died pretty soon after), the new spotlight on the issue of land acquisition made people realize it was in truly short supply, causing the trend to switch from indentured servitude to America's biggest fuckup: slavery. America began slavery with a lot of precedent, as the European shitheads they once mingled with had been doing it for years. Nobody really felt bad about it (or at least nobody felt bad enough to put up a fight). Most slaves ended up in the South, where low skill labor, like harvesting crops, was more common and more necessary, and due to the drastic number of slaves in the area, colonies like Carolina had to develop very strict laws to keep them from rebellion.

The Atlantic "Triangular" Trade System developed to satisfy this new need for slaves amongst the colonists. New England sold their shit (lumber) to England, but England thought that most of the New Englanders' shit was shitty, so to get more money, the New Englanders sold food to English-owned islands for feeding slaves. Confused yet? The islands sold back molasses (along with droves of other shit) to the colonists, who turned it into rum. They sold this rum to Africans that would give other Africans up to slavery, the new slaves working to grow the food that would start the system all over again

As the colonies started to make more money, England decided to take more money. The Navigation acts, passed from 1651 to 1673, did just that by dictating that colonial trading ships had to have Brits constantly involved—at one point 3/4 of the crew of an American trade ship had to be British—but also that colonial ports couldn't be used for foreign trade and that some goods could only be sold to Britain. This was only the beginning of a new general theme for the colonies of Britain paying closer attention, and being way more fucking annoying because of it.

TL;DR Everyone had land disputes with Native-Americans, because everyone was trying to take land from Native-Americans. The English colonists realized they didn't have much land to give away to indentured servants, so they started doing slavery instead. Britain wanted in on the action.

COLONIES DEVELOP, ENGLAND GETS SCARED

After a bunch of this shit started going down, England realized that they should probably, I don't know, actually take control of their colonies. It really didn't work that well, but in the end, the colonies ended up with governors and legislatures, so some good came out of it.

While each colony was unique, all the colonists were unified in their surprise at this sudden exertion of royal power. King James II stepped in and got his hands dirty in America, adopting Massachusetts, New Jersey, and the Carolinas as royal colonies, in 1691, 1702, and 1729, respectively.

Jimbo went kinda psycho from the power and suspended some of the charters for colonies (took power away from the original colonists and gave it to himself), but soon did a 180 and restored the charters after he quit drinking, I guess. Alongside English problems at home, dangerous shit was going down in Puritan New England, where a fuck ton of smuggling which was messing up all the English trading regulations. Jimmy boy handled this by creating the "Dominion of New England" in 1686. This group oversaw everywhere from New Jersey to Maine, and pissed off tons of colonists by kinda-sorta taking away the independence many colonies had been founded upon. It was run by Sir Edmund Andros, who had way too much power. Back in England, other pissed off people revolted in a Glorious Revolution (apparently) in 1688 which dethroned James II. So everyone was mad.

The colonists caught wind of what was going on in Britain, and they liked the idea so they started to rebel too. They somehow overpowered Andros and threw him in jail, and decided after they had their fun to become loyal to William and Mary, the ones who took the throne from King James. To the colonists' surprise, Will and Mary (while less insane) were greedy and regulatory just like James, so they fucked up New England traditions even more by issuing more charters.

On top of all of this, New England had to fight another goddamned war. This one was King William's War and was, imagine your surprise, against the French and the Natives that they were allied with from 1689 to 1697. Seriously, what the fuck, guys?

TL;DR The colonists let off some steam against the old British government (while the British people overthrew it) and then got monumentally fucked by the new British government.

All these revolutions and wars and shit culminated in the (in)famous Witchcraft Trials of 1692. Apparently it was "dark magic" to have actual skill/be a decent human being, so people wanted to burn "witches" at stake for anything from looking at them the wrong way to owning a better cook book. Strangely enough, a lot of the time people believed these accusations and got scared enough to kill a bunch of innocent "witches." Like the accused, the Salem Witch Hunt was short lived, and ended for three main reasons: 1. Because religion really had all the power, ministers had some say in whether or not this was going on. Turns out religious leaders don't like burning their followers alive for no reason. 2. Some royal charter was implemented. I guess it said you couldn't burn civilians anymore? 3. A lot of people in power were accused of being witches, so they decided to use all that power to shut the trials down.

After the whole burning thing stopped, people decided to kinda settle with the new rule, but many people still hated it to hell and back. Then another war broke out (Queen Anne's War) and colonists were asked to help because they'd apparently get some land or power or something. England wanted to do anything to get those colonists of their backs.

TL;DR Basically the Salem Witch Trials happened then people got distracted by war.

The 1700s: Let's Make A 'Merica!

(1700-1740) NOW WE HAVE CULTURE: DOUCHEBAG CULTURE, SURE. BUT STILL CULTURE

SHIT KINDA... STOPS BEING BAD? (FOR A DECADE)

Actually, for the first few decades of the 18th century (that means the 1700s, you're welcome), local colonial politics were fairly stable thanks to the creation of—you guessed it—a new elite. They weren't half bad and kept everything under control, for the most part. In some areas they agreed and worked together (around Virginia), in others they butted heads and wanted to fucking kill each other still (around New York). Things got so heated that in 1733, a New York Journalist named J. Peter Zenger was actually put on trial for writing a criticism of government actions in the newspaper. "But wait, isn't free press a thing?" Ah, now hold on, it's not 1776 yet, so nobody gives a shit about the rules. They've been making this up as they go along. This whole situation set a precedent for free press, though, because the Zenger case didn't end up getting anybody into real trouble, and Peter was quickly released from trial.

Another notable political change was the shift in power from the colony governors to assemblies. Despite this promotion, the assemblies didn't really pass anything, they just focused on trying to to protect people's rights and shit from the governors. The people started to see this system paralleling that of the English government, which it kinda was, but at the time that was still considered a healthy process to mirror in many colonists' minds, so the shift was all-in-all more comforting than concerning.

The development wasn't just political either. Populations grew, and got more diverse (diversity will eventually piss people off, but overall it's a good thing for America), cities became more important and as they improved, they became not just a place for the dirt poor to toil, but also a location for the rich to settle down and laugh at the poor people...the urban elite was starting to form. Economies started to bustle more and more and with them came upgrades in standard of living for

---

everyone. Everyone and everything was developing.

TL;DR No more political uprising, people are getting some freedoms (Zenger case), and governors don't have as much power. 1 point for liberty.

BRAIN EXPAND: EDUCATION AND INTELLECTUALISM

As the 18th century went along its merry fucking way, more and more groups of elites were developing (starting to sound like a broken record?) and they were separated from the common rabble mainly by their education, use of leisure time for...actual leisure, and their knowledge of the European movement that became known as "the Enlightenment." It pushed for a belief in rationality and sciencey shit.

When the Enlightenment came to America, it gave the elite some sort of commonality and gave colleges more topics to teach about. Science, law, medicine, and higher mathematics became part of the education system. Somehow we went wrong along the way and now we have god-forsaken AP US History.

John Locke was a big fan of Enlightenment and wrote the *Two Treatises of Government* in 1691. It basically said that men had power over the governments that "rule" them and opposed the concept of divine right (religious people getting power 'cause GOD SAID SO).

Enlightenment ideals had a lot of effect on political and educational life, but the era was truly important because of its scientific advances, like the development of new treatments for smallpox, that could help the entire population. The Enlightenment lasted from about fifteen years before the 1700s, when everyone stopped being religious fanatics, to about fifteen years after the 1700s, when everyone got bored of science and started being religious fanatics again.

TL;DR People became enlightened to the fact that relying solely on religion for life was bullshit. They called it "the

Enlightenment". The enlightened had a hard on for knowledge, and also were kinda dicks to the non-enlightened. Overall the whole "lets actually use science to solve our problems" thing did more good than bad though.

RELIGION IS STILL POPULAR: PEOPLE ARE WOKE

Catchphrases aside, the Great Awakening happened from the 1730s to the 1760s, and was a religious revivalism movement. But let's be real here, it's the 18th century, religion never went away. Because the Enlightenment popped up, someone felt like they needed to fuck over all the smart people, and it came down to the church to do so. This revival was anti-Enlightenment because it really emphasized feelings over all that "rational bullshit" - John Edwards, probably.

Reverend John Edwards started the religious movement in New England in 1734-5, when he observed that colonial youth reacted well to the Calvinist message, that people got "saved" by surrendering to God completely...kinky.

George Whitefield picked it up after that and became the first televangelist from the Church of England. Televisions obviously weren't invented yet, so he just kinda walked around and preached shit. His bold messages unified a bunch of people, but in doing so caused a sectionalization in religious beliefs at the same time. Somehow, though, people became more tolerant after this. If too much different shit is going on, it gets pretty hard to stay focused on being angry at people for being into all the different shit.

TL;DR Sike there are still some religious fanatics but they calmed down...okay they're still screaming shit about God-knows-what (pun intended) but they're not killing people.

SOCIETES HAVE CULTURE: SHOCKER!

Many people were fucking dumb at this point in American history (the 1700s) and generally couldn't read, so ideals of the enlightenment were spread mostly orally (lol). Culture in turn developed through this oral tradition, creating communal and very local regions that stayed fairly confined.

Since colonies couldn't form an overarching culture between themselves, they turned back to the church to unite them. At this point, you really shouldn't be surprised by that. Attending church became the most important ritual to communal life and it almost became like a cult. Almost like organized religion is just a shit-ton of people standing in a room "talking" to their imaginary friend...Anyway.

Civic rituals also became popular throughout the colonies, to do basically what church events did with slightly less God. In New England, some colonies declared thanksgiving days as well as days of fasting and prayer. Militia-training days somehow also brought the community closer together.

Down south the civic rituals generally relied on court and election days. Hell knows what that means.

And to unite the two areas, people came from all over to witness the public punishment of criminals.

At the time, a new ritual also emerged. This was the "ritual of consumption" where everybody got tuberculosis and fucking died. Wait, no... Oh yeah, consumption as in shopping, not the debilitating disease. This is where the custom was born to buy cool shit and show it off. We still do that today, except with less Bibles and more...Supreme.

Gift-giving rituals became common between the colonists and the natives. The Colonists got some rum and gave the natives...uhhh... The rest is history.

TL;DR Americans in the 1700s began to do slightly creepier and sometimes cooler version of what Americans do today. On the bright side, they'd go on militia training days instead of playing Fortnite. On the darker side, some days they just agreed to not eat as a team building exercise. America has always been some fucking weirdos.

FAMILIES ARE IMPORTANT TOO... PLEASE COME BACK MOM

Diversity! It's a great word to throw around all the time with no elaboration whatsoever. Just read a college brochure. Now let's take a second to actually talk about how different types of families were changed by America in the 18th century.

- Native-American: Natives experienced dramatic changes in their family life due to disease and the pressure of Europeans (obviously). Extended families thus became even more important than they already were.

- Mixed Race: Sometimes in the backcountry of colonies, there were few European women, so mixed race families appeared. These families often took refuge in native villages, and their acceptance wavered depending on where they were.

- African-American: Usually African-American families existed as part of the European households. There weren't all too many blacks in the North, and the families were pretty dispersed in the South. Despite this, wide networks formed and many groups united against excessive punishment and slavery in general.

- European: Back in the 1700s, there were a shit-ton of people in families and they included every inhabitant of the house. Households worked as a kind of business to create goods for use or sale, then the head of the house would represent them and sell the goods to the outside world. Many families thrived through agriculture, and we hadn't discovered relative equality yet, so specific tasks were given to men and women. If there weren't kids, slaves or servants would be brought in. This proves that children are replacements for slaves and I will be bringing this issue up to the Child Protective Services. On top of the racial differences, family life in the city was also different than life in the country. While people in the country worked their asses off to make shit, people in the city went to marketplaces to sell shit that other people made. Also there was more contact with the outside world in the cities due to newspapers, ports, and the like.

TL;DR Families in the 1700s, whether of different races or different geography, all had experiences that were actually diverse. Slaves were often blended into European families as workers, highly degraded but also somewhat included.

(1740-1770) ENGLAND'S FAVORITE PASTIME: PISSING OFF THE COLONISTS

POLITICS HEATS UP AGAIN

By the 1740s, all that bubbling tension finally caught up to colonial society, and crises erupted left and right like it was the 7th grade science fair. People were once again pissed at the lack of accommodations that the last revolution got them, and sought out to get more by, once again, attacking whoever held more power than them.

The Stono Rebellion happened in 1739, in South Carolina. One fine morning, twenty slaves got together outside of Charlestown and stole some guns and ammo from a store, killed the storekeeper and some families in the area, then fled to Florida. It didn't quite work out how they wanted it to, though, as they were captured and laws against blacks became

even harsher in light of their rebellion. Institutionalized racism sucks, but it gets worse when people piss off the institutions.

After the Stono Rebellion (and King George's War, which we'll get into later), white people went batshit against anyone who wasn't white. Many believed in the New York Conspiracy, where whites suspected that a biracial gang was going to start a slave uprising. I guess nothing really came out of it, though. Unless you count the entire Northern half of the country a hundred years later as a "gang."

The heat stayed on with the 1765-66 Land Riots of New (Jersey/York), that happened because a bunch of shitheads started illegally living on lands that were rented out to paying tenants. One family sued and got support from the courts, so the shitheads rebelled for a year or so, blah blah blah, people suck.

The Regulator Movements happened in the Carolinas too. That was just Scottish and Irish farmers rebelling against the local government because they thought they didn't have enough influence, governmental policy was unfair, and they were doing a really shitty job at law and order. The government eventually agreed with them just enough to appease the backcountry farmers, and in 1769, (lol) the Circuit Court Act was passed, which provided six new court districts for their rural habitat.

Around the 1750s and 60s, colonists got up off their asses and started giving a shit about British politics too. I guess they figured it was about time, since, y'know, Britain was literally fucking ruling them. The lead up really began with the Seven Years War. Or King George's War. Or the French and Indian War. Seriously guys, keep the fuck up with your naming.

TL;DR in the 1740s and 1760s people started to get heated about shit and rebel. It started with slaves and ended with farmers. The general theme: people who have nothing have nothing to lose.

THE SEVEN YEARS WAR OR WHATEVER YOU WANT TO CALL IT

Before the war, there was the Albany Congress in June of 1754, in which some delegates from some colonies got together and tried to: 1. Convince the Iroquois to join them (because they used their neutrality against everyone) and 2. Coordinate colonial defenses. Neither goal was met because bureaucracy is shit.

The war began, rather informally, in July 1754, when a new officer at the time, George Washington, attacked the French at Fort Necessity in modern day Pennsylvania. For the first time, the French kicked his ass and he eventually surrendered, but all in all this really was just the beginning of a much bigger conflict.

The British, under General Braddock, wanted to get the filthy baguette-lovers out of their land, but they ended up getting their asses handed to them on a silver platter by the French and the Natives. They did succeed, however, in getting the French out of Nova Scotia...so, I guess that's a win?

In 1756, shit got so bad that England and France actually declared war on each other in Europe. Things still were crap in America, though, because the British and the colonists still wanted each others balls on a pike. However, in 1757, William Pitt (the new Secretary of State) eased tensions and encouraged colonists to join the fight by promising that the British would refund the colonies for their losses. Given the trend, we can only assume that didn't go through very well.

In 1763, France surrendered and the Treaty of Paris (not the Peace of Paris) said that the French lost all their land in North America. That obviously didn't actually happen right away, but it was still nice to hear as a colonist, after watching friends die in a war for a country that you risked your lives to leave.

TL;DR The British use the colonists to fight off the French. It leads to a bunch of new problems for the colonists to deal with.

At the end of the war, Britain had 1) a larger empire, 2) a larger debt, and 3) a larger hate for the colonists. Well whaddya know, the war also made the colonists hate the British more! Both held each other in contempt during the war, and it kept hold after the war, too.

Shit kept going down with the Natives too, and Pontiac's Rebellion (1763, led by Pontiac) united a bunch of tribes because they felt that the colonist's spread across their land was concerning as fuck. They were defeated by the colonists, but the shaken British issued the Proclamation Line of 1763 regardless, which basically said the colonists couldn't settle past a certain point. I'll let you guess how well that worked out.

TL;DR Answer: it didn't work out.

ENGLAND SCRAMBLES LIKE AN EGG TO GET THEIR SHIT TOGETHER

So this is actually the second time the British "reorganized." The first was all that annoying "Dominion of New England" shit. The one from like the late 17th century to the Glorious Revolution? Doesn't matter.

What does matter is four pieces of legislation passed by Georgie Grenville (not actually named Georgie) between 1763 and 1765. These ones are fun cuz they got the colonists real pissed.

- Sugar Act (1764): More taxes, stronger anti-smuggling stuff. Colonies finally realized that this is put in place to make revenue, not as a fair tax.

- Currency Act (1764): Colonial paper money was banned for trade because the British needed the paper for teabags. To be fair, the money did change in value a lot, but shit hit the fan for colonial traders when they found out their money was worthless.

- Quartering Act (1765): Further raises colony taxes to provide shelter and housing for British soldiers.

- Stamp Act (1765): Talk about a shitstorm. Taxed all printed goods and materials. Hit the elite like a brick in the head because of how much paper they use. Also, stamps needed to be paid in sterling. Silver, I guess?

As noted, colonists would get extremely pissed off by these new Acts, and their reaction sparked the start of the beginning of the commencement of the first parts of the revolutionary war. It took time.

TL;DR The British started treating the colonists more shittily after sending them off the war, which got the colonists thinking about how much they didn't enjoy being treated like shit.

HOLD ON NOW, WHERE'S OUR REPRESENTATION?

England and the colonists believed in different theories of representation. George Grenville thought that Parliament ruled over all English subjects regardless of where they lived. Overcompensating for something there Georgie? On the other hand, the colonists thought they needed people to specifically represent their region, not just some random British Parliament members making all the calls. Thus was born the ideology called "Real Whigs" which basically said that a good government left their people (and their people's shit) alone and didn't get all up in their fucking business. This ideology spread like AIDS in the 80s as colonists realized that their English overlords weren't afraid to tax the hell out of them, without so much as asking their opinion on a new tax. In both scenarios, everyone was getting fucked in the ass; but the colonists, for all their flaws, were gearing up to do something about it.

TL;DR The colonists are pissed because they just feel like Britain just doesn't listen or care anymore. :((just like Valerie goddamn it Valerie you have to give us gentlemen gamers a chance you'll never get the love you need from some Chad.)

CURRENCY AND SUGAR ACTS ARE VERY UNPOPULAR

The economy was already in a depression due to the war in Europe. Now the Currency and Sugar Acts, two British money making schemes, fucked it all up even more. Still, people couldn't find the motivation to get organized. Eight different colonial legislatures all sent hate mail to Parliament and all eight failed.

TL;DR Europe bad, America not good.

THE STAMP ACT THO... YIKES

Wow. When the Stamp Act was passed it did seem really hopeless. Then Patrick Henry in the Virginia House of Burgesses got super hammered one night and wrote the Virginia Stamp Act Resolves (disclaimer: there is no historical evidence as to whether or not Mr. Henry drank alcohol while writing this and his lawyer will deny it in court). The Resolves were passed only after the really extreme parts were taken out. I guess they didn't appreciate Patrick calling Georgie a "two-faced snake-ass bitch" approximately 72 times. After the edits, it just reasserted the fact that the colonists were still British citizens — citizens who had the right to "consent to taxation". The colonists wanted some independence and rights, but not fully. Not yet. Pat's a real tease when he's drunk.

Meanwhile, the colonies were trying to find some sort of self-governing system while still remaining British subjects. "Nice try fucko" - Parliament. Organizations began to form, though, such as the:

- Loyal Nine: A Boston social club that held a demonstration including the lower classes. They hung an effigy of the local stamp guy and made him promise just not to do his job, basically. Another demonstration was targeted at the Governor, Thomas Hutchinson. Nothing too important happened.

- Sons of Liberty: An intercolonial group that attempted to influence political events... They could never actually control anything, though.

By 1766, the Sons of Liberty became a full-fledged force not to fuck with, there was a non-importation agreement by merchants, and the Stamp Act Congress met in New York to make some resolves (Almost). America, fuck yeah! Stuffs getting done.

TL;DR The stamp act really pissed people off, and America tried to figure out with eventual results how to balance being independent of Britain and...dependent on them.

TOWNSHEND AND THE STORY OF BAD TO WORSE

In March of 1766, Parliament finally repealed the Stamp Act because Lord Rockingham became Prime Minister instead of Grenville. Woo-hoo. He didn't believe in the law, but he did believe in the right to tax colonists, which made him a pretty basic shithead. What made him an even bigger Brit-head (see what I did there) was the Declaratory Act. This basically just meant: Fuck you, we're England! We can tax you if we want!

Then William Pitt got sick or something and new-age Brit-head Charles Townshend came into power somewhere. Either way, he imposed some new taxes for the colonies to try out.

The Townshend Acts were passed in 1767 and taxed trade goods (paper, glass, tea, lead, and stuff) imported from Britain and also were designed to raise money to pay the salaries of royalty and their officials. Fuck off Charles.

TL;DR New Brit-heads came to power and were about as dicky as the last ones. Especially Charles Townshend.

COLONIAL RESPONSE. TRY AND GUESS HOW THIS TURNS OUT

Absolutely no hesitation. Essays were written, but probably the most important and the one you actually learn about is *Letters from a Farmer in Pennsylvania* by John Dickinson. He said basically that Parliament could regulate colonial trade, but not tax it just to bring in revenue.

A second movement of non-importation was led by the Daughters of Liberty. Even before America was formed it was still trying to prove it's not sexist. The boycotts weren't completely followed by everyone, but they were still effective. In April 1770, the Townshend taxes were repealed, except for the tea one for some reason. The Acts themselves were still in place, but it really didn't matter now.

TL;DR Americans got their act together to get rid of a bunch of other Acts.

(1770-1774) FORESHADOWING THE REVOLUTION: LET'S PISS OFF THE COLONISTS EVEN MORE!

SHOOTY SHOOTY BANG BANG IN BOSTON

Five civilians were killed in Boston the same day that the Prime Minister proposed repealing the Townshend taxes. Surprisingly it didn't have anything to do with the political shitheads in England at the time, just good old fashioned American violence.

Some customs people came to Boston a while before all the Townshend mess and mobs started to fuck their shit up. Soldiers had to be assigned to protect them, long story short a snowball fight turned into a shootout and now the colonists have metaphorical ammo for patriotism. This event would come to be known as the "Boston Massacre" though it was really closer to a snowball fight. Everything got hyped up cause people hated the Brits. A Black Northerner, Crispus Attucks, was the first of the five to be killed in the skirmish, making March 5th, 1770 the first day of the revolution and Attucks the first casualty.

TL;DR Bostonian winters can get really heated sometimes.

TWO YEARS OF SUSPICION AND SIDE-EYEING

From 1770 to 1772, everything was weirdly calm. Newspapers still published articles shit-talking the British, but no one really wanted true independence yet. Patriots were still like "eh, we're British subjects I guess..." but made systems to govern themselves and still remain loyal to the King. Guess what, Parliament didn't like that one bit. Whatever, though. Shit was still alright.

Until, of course, the fall of 1772, when some British asshats began implementing the part of the Townshend Acts that said that governors could be paid from customs revenues. The colonists told them to fuck off by creating the Committee of Correspondence, led by good ol' Sam Adams in Boston, that was tasked with gathering publicity for patriotism, especially the "British people suck" kind.

TL;DR 1770-1772 was the calm before the storm. Then came the storm of British people being dicks. Sorry, was that insensitive? I meant to say British people being *willies.*

BOSTON SPILLS THE TEA

By the time 1773 rolled around, only the tea part of the Townshend shit was still in effect. Some people were still boycotting it, but most people just said fuck it. Then Britain had the absolutely brilliant idea of making the Tea Act in May 1773 to save the East India Co. from bankruptcy.

Basically, the East India tea was the only legal tea in America, but sold directly into the colonies. The tea was actually cheaper, but it was still seen as a "taxing" act by Britain. Eh, double pun? No? Fuck off.

Anyway, this led to the Boston Tea Party on December 16, 1773, where about 10,000 pounds (the currency ones) of tea were dumped into the water by early revolutionists. America! We're really proud of this, though what it really led to was Britain closing the Boston Harbor and America not really solving much.

TL;DR Britain made a tax that made tea slightly cheaper for Americans, so naturally we went overboard with their tea (pun intended).

ALMOST THERE...

Britain obviously is seeing red from the Tea Party, so they pass some more ass- backwards Acts, like the Coercive Acts, in 1774. These included:

- Port Bill: The port of Boston was shut down until the tea was repaid in full. Talk about setting an example...

- Government Act: Annulled the Massachusetts Charter and fucking wrecked all colonial legislative power. Severely limited all town meetings as well.

- Quartering Act (again?): Now forced colonial assemblies to build some barracks or have the soldiers live with

---

residents. I thought my roommate was bad enough.

- Administration of Justice Act: Any soldier who killed a colonist was allowed to be tried in a British court. So basically they get away with FUCKING MURDER.

- Also the Quebec Acts, which allowed Catholicism in previously French territories and allowed the French to go past the Declaration Line, into the Ohio River Valley. Fuckwads.

The colonists finally had their worst fears confirmed, and all the colonies agreed to meet in Philly in September 1774 for the Continental Congress...

TL;DR British people got pissed off by the colonists, so they pissed the colonists off even more. They're really screwed now.

(1774-1783) WE MADE IT! THE REVOLUTIONARY WAR

1774-75, BRITISH AUTHORITY SHITS ITSELF

So the Continental Congress met on September 5 and had three goals:

- Define American general grievances (Star W*rs jokes are funny?).

- Develop a resistance plan (Star Wars still?)

- Define their constitutional relationship with Britain (I've got nothing for this one)

After a lot of unintelligible yelling, probably, John Adams came up with the idea to only obey Parliament when they thought doing so would be best for America and Britain. Good idea I guess, but does it work? Who knows.

They also wanted the Coercive Acts repealed (who wouldn't) and would start an economic boycott AND petition the king at the same time. It's like when your wife's boyfriend buys you a new XBox for your birthday but then refuses to help you set it up.

Anywho, the Continental Association was implemented from late 1774 until early 1775, and consisted of no importation of British goods, no consumption of British products, and no exportation of American goods to Britain.

At the same time regular colonial governments were being fucked over by patriots challenging their authority through popularly elected provincial conventions. If you have any idea what that means, please explain it to me, because I have no fucking clue. Either way, it was shit for royal officials. It doesn't matter unless you're really THAT into history, in which case you should've bought a more expensive book.

TL;DR Americans decided to listen to Britain only when it was convenient to them...mixed results to be expected.

THE FIRST BATTLE OF THE BRITISH-PEOPLE-SUCK-AND-THEIR- ISLAND-SHOULDN'T-COUNT-AS-A-COUNTRY WAR

The actual fighting began on April 19, 1775, when General Tommy Gage in Boston sent an expedition to take some colonial military supplies in Concord. One Paul Revere heard about this, he rode a horse around screaming about it for a bit, and everyone got hot and bothered about the whole thing. There was a skirmish at Lexington, which was on the way, then the British got attacked at Concord itself.

———

The Brits got pushed back, and for the year following Concord, the colonial troops sieged Boston. The red-coated idiots finally broke away at the Battle of Bunker Hill, but a lot of their troops died in the process.

TL;DR The Battles at Lexington and Concord started the Revolutionary War; So far, the Americans were literally killing it.

THE BRITISH DIDN'T HAVE A CLUE WHAT THEY WERE DOING. DID THE AMERICANS?

The British Prime Minister, Lord North, made three main assumptions about this war:

• Patriot forces can't win against British troops (idiot).

• War in America is the same as war in Europe (IDIOT).

• Winning the war would make the colonies come back to Britain (I D I O T).

So yeah, all three of those things are wrong. They didn't realize the sheer amount of political (not only military) force it would take to get the colonies back with them and also just how committed colonial forces were in this war. Arrogant Brit-heads.

On the other side, Americans had the home field advantage. And in war, it makes an even bigger difference than in sports. Their people fought harder because they were actually fighting for THEIR FUCKING LAND...(well, the land they stole from the Natives). They also had easier access to supplies and their generals were actually willing to work well together, unlike the bumbling Brits.

However, there were some obstacles to the colonies effort. They didn't have a big, sprawling bureaucracy to organize a war like Britain did; all they had was the Second Continental Congress. Even so, that was really only supposed to be a brief meeting when it started and ended up becoming the assembly that made up the American government. Oh well. This did allow America to form an official Continental Army, though, with George Washington as its general.

What really gave the colonies the advantage wasn't even part of the colonies. The necessity of French support would be an embarrassment to most founding fathers. Except Jefferson of course, who would have trouble keeping it in his pants at the mere sound of the accent. Speaking of Jefferson...

TL;DR The British underestimated America...and America's connection to France, leaving the door open to what would become a successful revolution.

THOMAS JEFFERSON INVENTS AMERICA

Even though we were fighting, Americans were still "eh" on independence. But then Thomas Paine (probably his wrestling name tbh) released a book called "Common Sense" which made everyone reassess their views of colonial relationships to Britain. I actually read it, and it was just one page that said "It's common fucking sense, dude."

Because of that, independence was pretty much decided upon by late spring 1776. On May 10, the Second Continental Congress proposed making state constitutions. Then on June 7 (my roommate's birthday!) they made a motion towards independence. It was postponed until July, where some people were gathered to draft a...declaration...Sound familiar? Anyway, Tommy J told King George to suck a fat one and now we're free. Good times.

TL;DR Thomas Jefferson wrote the Declaration of Independence of 1776 because Thomas Paine convinced everyone we needed it. Points for the Thomases.

———

- 1776-1777: Containment in New England. British assholes just thought this was a radical minority movement centralized in New England. Then the battle of Bunker Hill happened, in which they ate shit and choked on their words.

- 1777-1778: The Middle Colonies. After a sufficient amount of shit was eaten, Britain moved to the middle colonies to try to gain the Hudson River and Mohawk Valley. Then they lost at Saratoga and that colonial victory caused France to join our cause and give us a big helping hand. The British gave up and moved to...

- 1778-1781: The South. Britain took Charlestown, but the French dicked them with their big boats. The last stages of the war were just Britain frantically running around trying to do something until General Cornwallis surrendered to Washington at Yorktown in 1781.

- 1783: The Official Treaty. Ben Franklin led the negotiations and signed it on September 3, 1783, walking out with an officially recognized independent nation with borders from Canada to Florida and from the Mississippi to the Atlantic. We didn't get Canada like we wanted, but we did get some fishing privileges in Newfoundland. So we signed the Treaty of Paris and got a country. A pretty good deal if you ask me.

TL;DR In a geographic sense, the war was the British Army going down on the colonies...or south. Whatever you wanna call it. Either way, we ended up winning.

(1776-1789) WHO WOULD WIN: SOME ARTICLES OF CONFEDERATION OR ONE CONSTITUTION BOI

REPUBLICS ARE A THING

Most Americans felt that the new country should be a Republic, and that its citizens should be "virtuous" or whatever to bolster the stability of said republic, but of course, there were three different interpretations of what all this (Republicanism) meant:

- One view was held by some of the elite who wanted a small, homogenous society where citizens would sacrifice their personal shit for the good of the whole. This would create a merit-based "natural" aristocracy.

- A second view was held by some skilled craftsmen and the rest of the asshole elite who focused more on economics, focusing on Adam Smith and his theories about self- interest helping the community. They basically said if everyone followed their private interests there'd be "republican virtue".

- The third was held by less educated people and radicals who wanted more participation in government to give people a say.

TL;DR All versions of Republicanism had substantially different messages, but were the same in the fact that they said "Fuck Britain." America would turn out O.K. after all.

BUT GOOD ONES ARE HARD TO MAKE

Everyone saw these ideas and was like "all right, but the people need to be good, right? Do we have good people? Who cares, let's just make some people believe whatever we think is right so they vote the same way as us." So artists, educators, and politicians tried to bang some values into people's heads.

Artists had a hard time with this. Many art pieces were examples of corruption and luxury, something we didn't want. At this point, though, artists made conscious efforts to show virtue and patriotism in their works.

William Hill Brown wrote *The Power of Sympathy* in 1789 to basically tell women to shut their legs and get some education...not as controversial at the time, and Royall Tyler wrote *The Contrast* in 1787, a play that basically shit on Americans who acted *too* British.

Education really picked up and two major changes were put in place: 1) some northern states took more money from citizens in the form of taxes to pay for elementary schools and 2) schooling was improved for women. Judith Murray fought for women's education and said that men and women were equally intelligent, but the lack of education made women appear dumber. Now, in 2018, we actually know that women are often smarter than most men (except the two men who tricked you into buying this weird ass book. We're smarter than all of you, regardless of gender.)

Women's roles were also rethought, Abigail Adams even piping in to write a letter campaigning for equal rights, and saw about as much success as most women did in the day. At least now some women were educated enough to read what she said.

TL;DR All that Revolution shit got us thinking. Maybe we should have some schools? Maybe women should even have some rights? These were really provocative questions at the time.

EH-MANCIPATION: SOME PEOPLE GET FREEDOM

Now, you guys know the Civil War happened, right? Cool. Well, this is before the Civil War, so slavery is still an issue.

The north began a process of "gradual emancipation" in 1777, when Vermont abolished slavery. In the 1780s, Massachusetts followed suit. Pennsylvania did it in 1780 and New Jersey in 1804.

The south couldn't give any less of a shit though, and they obviously kept it. There was no question whatsoever. At least by the slave owners living there.

The number of free blacks did grow even before any emancipation due to freedom during war, serving in the war, or being freed by their owners. They migrated north, but emancipation didn't bring equality, and discrimination was as present in the North as slavery in the South. The free blacks had to form their own institutions in the North and gradually began a new life as a free but degraded people.

Southerners were fucked when it came to, you know, actual reasoning behind why they were still keeping slaves, so they made a theory. Instead of stating that the slaves were inferior because of the environment, they just went all out and said that they were "less than fully human." Fuck's sake, guys. Some even said that being enslaved protected and helped the otherwise "incompetent" unwilling immigrants.

This is actually when "race" became attributed to skin color. Really. Southern slavery was a unifier for both blacks and whites, and many whites started characterizing all blacks under certain traits (lazy, dishonest, etc.).

From the start, the Republic (in the South, if not some of the North too) was a really great place to be, unless you weren't a white male.

TL;DR The North started to end slavery, the South?...we'll get to them eventually. Even so, on both sides, the privilege of being white was apparent.

STATE GOVERNMENTS >>> PROVINCIAL CONGRESS

The Second Continental Congress, in May 1776, ordered states to make their own governments so they wouldn't just have to throw all their shit into the Congress to get it done.

(I'm gonna be honest, this part bored the actual shit out of me. No jokes for this section, this is gonna be straight up facts because fuck it.)

State constitutions had to be written by special conventions, which were then handed to voters in order to ratify them.

Basically, the state governments focused on the distribution and some limitation of government power. America, after dealing with Britain, didn't really like the idea of too much centralized authority. The governor, because of this, had very little independent authority, a limited term, but still expanded the legislative powers of state legislatures. The states were more focused on protecting citizens than making the government effective at this point, so much so that the governor had to be given more power after a while. Checks and balances were being theorized about, but didn't come around until the Constitution in 1787.

We done with that? Fucking finally.

TL;DR State governments come into play, and don't mean much at first, but they do help relax things for the national government as all this constitution business gets sorted.

NOT QUITE A CONSTITUTION

In 1777 someone had the absolutely genius idea of writing down the rudimentary agreements of the Continental Congress, and it accidentally became the Articles of Confederation. Anyway, what was in it?

- A one house legislative system where states could send delegates that would vote as a unit.

- What could it do? Declare war, make peace, sign treaties, borrow money, get bitches, organize a post office, establish some armed forces, smoke weed on their lunch break, issue bonds, manage lands, and get plastered every night.

- They needed 2/3 votes to pass legislation and a unanimous vote to make an amendment.

- There was no executive branch and no national judiciary branch. Also, it had no power   over state governments.

- No national currency because fuck that shit.

Some historians called this period (1781-1788) the Critical Period because the country was about to fucking shit itself. Others disagreed, but who cares, they're all dead now. No matter what you think, there were definitely some problems. And a lot of them came from this half-assed version of the constitution

TL;DR The Continental Congress and the Articles of the Confederation were the law of the land for a few years, but they would be ineffective in the long run and needed to be replaced.

THAT'S A LOT OF DAMAGE

There were problems. Finance was one of them. The legislature just tried printing some money because there was a high demand for goods. The American dollar inflated like that girl from Willy Wonka who turned into a blueberry, and by 1780, American money was as worthless as an opinion from someone who likes socks and sandals. Next came economic "warfare" between states, competing to sell the same shit all their neighbor states were selling, which just drove us further in the shitter.

The weak national government affected foreign trade, because the Articles said Congress didn't have the power to establish a commercial policy. Cheap foreign goods flooded our markets, causing a drop in domestic prices and hurting merchants and farmers. At this point, that was basically everyone. Now our economy became even more worthless, like the opinion of someone with an anime profile pic.

We couldn't deal with the Spanish at our southern borders, either, and we couldn't negotiate our way out of a paper bag. So, tough luck, the Mississippi River was closed in 1784. (We also couldn't enforce treaties according to the Articles, so we couldn't do much about the Treaty of Paris, and had to let Britain kept their forts on the Western frontier).

TL;DR The Articles of Confederation put a very vanilla American government into some hardcore bondage. It wasn't comfortable for anyone, and as kinky as inflation sounds, the economy wasn't buying it. (both puns intended)

SPEAKING OF WESTERN FRONTIERS

After the Treaty of Paris, we assumed we'd get everything east of the Mississippi. We forgot about the natives.

We tried to negotiate throughout the 1780s in the North, but by 1790 New York State had already bought a bunch of land from individual Iroquois nations and we moved in before you could say "manifest destiny".

In the Southwest we sent some settlers into native lands, but this provoked the Creek tribe. Oops. Anyway, we got into a war that didn't end until 1790. Good, patriotic, American shit.

We made some ordinances for settling the Northwest Territories. This included the Mississippi River area, the Great

Lakes, and the Ohio River boundaries.

The Land Ordinances of 1784-85 described the process by which public land could become private. 1) An area would be divided into more than 4, but less than 7, states. 2) The area would be surveyed into 36 square mile areas, each of which would be surveyed into 36 townships (side note, I still don't know what it means to survey something, but we'll just say it means "divide it up"). 3) Territory ownership would be transferred to the federal government, who would then sell the land to individuals. 4) One of the 36 squares would be used to raise revenue for schools.

On a larger scale, The Northwest Ordinance of 1787 described the process by which territories would become states. 1) Every new state has the same rights as the original states. 2) Slavery could not be established in the area. 3a) A governor and 3 judges are appointed. 3b) If there are 5000 adult males, a territorial legislature can be created. 3c) If the population gets to 60,000, delegates can be elected to make a state constitution. If Congress approves it, it becomes a state.

TL;DR As obstacles to getting more land arose, America started thinking things through, and with the Land Ordinances of 1784-85 and the Northwest Ordinance of 1787, there were finally some set in stone processes for how American land could be claimed, reclaimed, and classified.

AMERICA HAS ITS FIRST CONVENTION

We soon realized that America (and especially Congress) could do fuck all under the Articles of Confederation and that we needed something new. Representatives from Virginia and Maryland met independently at Mount Vernon in March 1785 to discuss an agreement over trade on the Potomac River. That went well, so they called for a general meeting in

Annapolis in September 1786 to discuss trade. Only 5 delegations actually showed up, so they rescheduled for a new meeting in Philly.

Then Shays' Rebellion bitch-slapped everyone in the face and they decided they had better attend for real this time. Basically, Revolutionary War Veteran Daniel Shays and some farmers raided the Springfield armory in Massachusetts and said the government was tyrannical. Usual rebellion stuff. The Confederation failed to have any protocol for this kinda shit, so we we're left pretty much helpless to send in any government forces. That really convinced people to make a strong central government, so the Constitutional Convention was finally held in Philly in May 1787.

TL;DR When crazy farmers can fuck up your government, you realize it probably needs to be a little bit reformed. After Shays' rebellion, all the states agreed to replace the Articles of Confederation and now here we are with a Constitutional Convention!

BLAH BLAH BLAH PLANS BLAH BLAH BLAH CONSTITUTION

Ugh. More boring stuff.

Many of the delegates had similar ideas, but still disagreed over the minute details. Take, for example, the Virginia Plan and the New Jersey Plan:

- Virginia Plan: James Madison's idea. A bicameral legislature where the amount of representatives for each state would be proportional to their population, an executive branch elected by Congress, a national judiciary, and Congressional power over state laws.

- New Jersey Plan: A small-state response to the Virginia Plan with a unicameral legislature and the power to tax and regulate trade. Like the Articles of Confederation but stronger.

We eventually compromised, as per usual, and ended up with

what we have today. A bicameral legislature with one house going by population (the House of Representatives) and one house having two people per state (the Senate). Overall, more limited than the Virginia Plan, but more flexible than the New Jersey Plan.

A few people got everyone to quiet down and then yelled "BUT WHAT ABOUT SLAVES?" Needless to say, that irritated everyone quite a bit, but they realized the need to address the growing issue of slavery. Well, they didn't exactly address it, they just kinda acknowledged it was there without taking the time to solve anything. Southern states wanted slaves to count as part of the population, not out of any sort of respect for their personhood, but simply because it would get southern states, which had considerably more slaves, more representation in the House of Representatives. The compromise was that a slave would be counted as.... 3/5 of a person. Nice going fuckheads, you somehow became more racist.

Anywho, the Convention had its last meeting on the 17th of September, 1787, and now we just had to ratify the new Constitution.

TL;DR At the constitutional convention, we argued over two things: whether states of different populations should all have equal representation in Congress, and if not, whether slaves should count as a part of those populations. We compromised on both issues.

54 PAGES IN AND WE FINALLY GET A CONSTITUTION

The Constitutional Convention Comrades submitted the Constitution to the states, needing it to be ratified by special conventions in at least nine of them. Almost as soon as this was announced, America split into two parties faster than George Washington could give his farewell address.

- Federalists: Supported the Constitution, liked the merit-based aristocracy. No need to fear a strong central government if there was a separation of powers anyway.

- Anti-Federalists: First of all, what a great, original and creative name. Anyway, they thought that weakening the states would lead to oppressive government power. They were revolutionaries and farmers, not liking the central government shit. They also supported a Bill of Rights.

Federalists won because they gave in and supported a Bill of Rights too, and eventually ratification was celebrated on July 4, 1788. America, fuck yeah!

TL;DR At the Constitutional Convention, everyone was arguing over two things: whether states' Congressional representatives should be equal or proportional to population, and if proportional, whether slaves should be included in the population count. We compromised on both.

MAKING AN ACTUAL FUNCTIONING GOVERNMENT

The first Congress met in April 1789 and was composed mostly of Federalists. Imagine your surprise. Though pretty one-sided, the new Congress still had a lot of questions to deal with:

- Revenue: James Madison pushed the Revenue Bill of 1789, which put a 5% tariff on some imports. Good shit, Jimmy.

- The Bill of Rights: Jim took the helm again and wrote 19 amendments to the Constitution, 10 of which were ratified on December 15, 1791 and became known as the Bill of Rights. This really rallied support for the new government.

- Judiciary organization: This was taken care of by the Judiciary Act of 1789, which set up a 6 person Supreme Court, 13 district courts, and 3 courts of appeal. Whatever those are. Can I appeal for my wife to stop going on business trips with Chadwick? Anyway.

- Executive organization happened but it's nothing too important.

TL;DR First Congress Highlights: New Tariff, Bill of Rights, a Supreme Court, and so much more! Brought to you By James Madison, who did pretty much all the work.

(1789-1800) YOUNG AMERICA: GEORGE WASHINGTON DOES A REALLY GOOD JOB AND THEN EVERYONE IGNORES ALL OF HIS ADVICE

GEORGE RUNS A COUNTRY

After everything got set up, Revolutionary General (pun intended) George Washington was elected to be our first president. Boy would he be fucking proud to see how far we've come now, writing about him in a history book that just invented the word "dickassery". Aware of the shit to come, he was cautious, knowing he would be the guy people pointed to for everything. He was the president who set the precedents, highlights including his decision to not run for a third term (he didn't want anyone getting the idea that presidents should be in office for life) and cautioning citizens in his farewell address to avoid forming toxic political parties and getting America into entangling alliances with other countries.   Washington and his don't-fuck-this-up attitude went and chose the heads of the executive departments, as follows:

- War: Henry Knox

- Treasury: Alexander Hamilton

- State: Thomas Jefferson

- Attorney: Edmund Randolph

Remember some of them?

Hamilton is especially important, because he didn't give a shit about anyone else. So when Congress asked him to fix debt (because that's how countries work I guess), he came up with something just a tad controversial...

TL;DR George Washington tried to be a good, safe, vanilla president. Unfortunately he appointed a kinky narcissist, Alexander Hamilton, to be in charge of money. Lets see how that plays out.

YOU COULD WRITE A MUSICAL ABOUT THE GUY

So Alex Hamilton had a plan. A money plan, to be specific. Here are some bullet points about it:

- Report on Public Credit (1790): Congress should assume state debts, combine them with the national debt, then redistribute it equally throughout the states. Don't worry about how New York is 10,000 times larger than Rhode Island, it's fine. Madison objected this because it gave the central government too much power AND Virginia, Madison's home, had already paid off their debt. Those sneaky shits were trying to get out of it. In the end, though, Hamilton got the votes he needed in a series of compromises that somehow ended up deciding where the capital would be (On the Potomac River, if you were wondering).

- The Bank of the United States: Hamilton wanted to charter a national bank that would be capitalized at $10 million and funded by private investors. The bank would circulate currency and collect/lend money to/from the treasury. If you didn't take Economics, just know that this means a lot of power for a lot of people in power. Was that constitutional?

    ◦ Madison said no. If the Constitution doesn't say you can, then you can't. He had a strict Constructionist view.

    ◦ Hamilton (obviously) said yes. If the Constitution doesn't say you can't, then you can. Hamilton had a loose Constructionist view.

    ◦ In the end, Washington liked it, so the bank was passed.

- There was another protective tariff that was proposed but denied so why give a fuck.

- There was a tax on whiskey that's worth mentioning because it started the Whiskey Rebellion in Pennsylvania; Backcountry farmers who grew the shit you need to make whiskey started by protesting, but eventually things became violent in July 1794. The only thing that causes more violence than alcohol is taking it away. In August of the same year, Washington gathered some

13,000 militiamen and put a quick end to the pissy farmers' revolt. He demonstrated that the government, now with a Constitution instead of the weak ass Articles of Confederation, could and would get kick the shit out of people violently reacting to laws.

TL;DR The Constitution and people around it made some major changes to America. Hamilton started organizing money, and giving more of it to the national government, which was finally functional and funded enough to enforce the laws it had been making for years.

WE GET PARTIES... THE BAD KIND

Even though our theories said opposition was useless, in 1794 the Democratic- Republican party had formed in opposition to the Federalists. It was headed by Jefferson and Madison, who thought Hamilton was RKOing basic revolutionary ideals.

In response, Hamilton and his supporters were called the Federalists and said that the D-Rs were an illegal faction plotting against the government. People in power became bitches really fast, considering they just fought a war against other bitches in power.

Washington, still not trying to fuck this all up for himself, decided to stay neutral. When he got re-elected in 1792 he was promoting unity, then some foreign affairs came in and messed shit up. The Baguette People have arrived.

TL;DR People took sides, Hamilton and the Federalists now kinda fizzled away their Anti-Federalist opponents, and before they could pop open the champagne a new challenger was approaching: Jefferson, Madison, and the Democratic-Republicans. Washington wasn't having it.

HON HON HON IT IS US THE BAGUETTE PEOPLE (AND FOREIGN AFFAIRS)

In 1789, most Americans supported the now ongoing French Revolution. Then when it got bloodier, and France declared war on a bunch of European countries in 1793, we got cold feet about the whole situation.

We had the Treaty of Alliance with France from 1778, but we also had previous bonds with Britain and depended on their imports to sustain our economy; this was pretty much exactly the situation of entangling alliances Washington aimed to avoid. We eventually declared neutrality, but the D-Rs supported France very strongly. Hamilton was heated.

Meanwhile, Washington was actually tried to solve shit, and sent John Jay to London in order to negotiate away our four main issues with the British:

• Britain taking our ships/impressing our sailors. (Not impressing like "wow British guy your tea and ships and willies are so cool," but impressing as in "hey there American guy you're gonna be a British soldier now or we'll just take all your shit anyway."

• British forts that were still probably plotting some shit in the Northwest.

• A commercial treaty.

• Compensation for slaves that left with their army after the war. Somehow.

In the end, Jay's Treaty (1795) only dismantled some forts and got some trade restrictions. In exchange, England could have tariffs on American goods and their exports were favored by our merchants. We averted a war, but many Americans didn't like this, because they felt like they already sorta earned independence in the last war. We couldn't do shit about it, though, because the treaty was made and ratified in secret long before any angry citizens heard about its details.

We also organized a treaty with Spain, just for kicks, called Pinckney's Treaty, that gave us the ability to use the Mississippi River again. Woo.

TL;DR The Federalists and the Democratic Republicans take sides on France. Meanwhile, Washington tries to get Britain off our asses and Spain helps us out a little by letting us share the Mississippi River.

THE LINES ARE DRAWN

 The election of 1796 was drawing closer, and Jay's Treaty really showed the true colors of each political party. Federalists didn't like ordinary people getting involved in politics, had wet dreams about a strong central government, were pretty much Pro-Britain, and were just generally pessimistic asshats. Democratic-Republicans disliked the central government, wanted more westward expansion, preferred farming and shit to big cityfolk life (which at that time was just slightly more crowded and a lot less clean than farming), and were more optimistic about independence. The D-Rs slowly became the majority throughout the course of the 1790s.

As these two were fighting like children, the adult in the room was retiring. George Washington gave his farewell address, which should have been a wakeup call to pretty much everyone. He called for commercial—but not political—links to other countries (i.e. lets trade with everyone else but not make a bunch of "entangling alliances with them), unilateralism (i.e. let's try to all actually agree on something before we do it), and for unity (i.e. chill with the political parties or shit is gonna hit the fan).

Then the election itself rolled around. John Adams and Thomas Pinckney represented the Federalists and Thomas Jefferson and Aaron Burr represented the DRs. Electors were told to only pick their two favorites because the Constitution didn't account for parties, so Federalist John Adams became president with... Democratic Republican Thomas Jefferson as his vice president. Fuck.

TL;DR Washington retired and told people not to do a list of things he outlined as "stupid shit." Spoiler alert, they do all those things anyway. Things were gonna get even weirder, however, as the second president and his VP came from two different political parties.

ADAMS HAS NO FUCKING CLUE WHAT'S HAPPENING

Johnny thought largely in the same way that Washington did, basically that the president should be above politics, not supporting any factions. This led to people taking advantage of him and pretty much running the entire fucking country for him, leading to major inconsistency. Alas, as most people were focusing their efforts on domestic politics, Adams was left alone to deal with a brewing crisis abroad.

Jay's Treaty outraged the French, so, ever the reasonable ally, they started taking over American trade ships, which were often carrying British goods. In response, Adams sent three people over to negotiate with the thieves. Things got messy, there were bribe demands and a bunch of shady shit our new country couldn't afford to get involved with, so Adams told Congress it wasn't working. The jumpy-ass Congress assumed Adams was trying to sabotage the whole project, so they demanded he release the reports of the negotiations. Adams withheld the names of the French agents, so the uber-creative American public nicknamed this the "XYZ Affair" after the three unnamed negotiators, and since they couldn't blame any specific Frenchmen, they just stayed pissed at the entire country. Then Congress put the 1778 Alliance Treaty through a paper shredder and we had a semi-war in the Caribbean. Shit happens.

The D-Rs still supported France, and Adams had his thumbs up his ass trying to discern whether or not to call them traitors. The other Federalists, though, saw this as the perfect opportunity to prove the D-Rs were subverting the country. In 1798, the Federalist Congress passed the Alien and Sedition Acts, which were targeted at recent immigrants (who were usually D-Rs).

- The Naturalization Act lengthened the residency requirement to become a citizen and had all resident aliens registered.

- The Alien Acts allowed for the detainment of enemy aliens during wartime and allowed the president to deport dangerous aliens.

- The Sedition Act affected citizens as well and limited speech against the government. Typical Tuesday morning Federalist shit.

Adams then sent another envoy to Paris, seeking compensation for the lost ships and for the breaking of the 1778 treaty. France gave us fuck-all for the ships, but the Convention of 1800 did end that semi-war going on. However, the results of this weren't known until after the election of 1800, so the whole deal cost him the election. (Jumping forward a bit, the 12th amendment in 1804 changed voting to a party ticket, solving the Adams-Jefferson problem of the 1796 election)

TL;DR While the two parties handled shit at home, Adams fucked up his one job with the French, ironically giving his party the opportunity to make the D-R's look like dickheads.

HOLD ON FOLKS, RACISM ISN'T OVER YET

In 1789, when a bunch of natives came under our influence, Henry Knox wanted to... how should I put this... "civilize" them. The Indian Trade and Intercourse Act (not that kind you sick fuck) of 1793 realized this idea by saying the United States Government would give the natives animals, tools, and instructions for farming. Cool, I guess. But the bill still fucked over the native traditions, communal landowning, and generally disrespected their entire culture. Not like a single American gave a shit back then.

African-Americans were also adapting parts of general American culture to help their cause; this began religiously, with African-Americans forming their own Baptist and Methodist congregations. These congregations were sometimes used to plan revolts, like Gabriel's Revolt in 1800 and Sancho's Conspiracy. Don't ask me what either of those actually are. Neither of them actually worked, as both were found out, and they both resulted in stricter laws against slaves. They couldn't catch a break.

TL;DR The U.S. Gov forced African-Americans to solve their own problems, and forcibly "solved" "problems" they claimed Native-Americans needed solved.

The 1800s: Because Fuck Poor People

(1800-1816) ENGLAND TO AMERICA: "STOP HITTING YOURSELF, STOP HITTING YOURSELF, STOP HITTING YOURSELF"

THE "REVOLUTION" OF 1800

Welcome to 1800. Both sides hate each-other in this election, the Democratic- Republicans backing Jefferson and the Federalists trying to re-elect Adams, but nonetheless, power was once again peacefully replaced. The "revolution" comes from the fact that this election ushered in a new era of power for the Democratic-Republican party.

Jefferson had been a pretty productive and drama-free president. He didn't look to abolish the national bank like some extremists in his party wanted, as he wasn't ready to piss off all the Federalists he had once worked side-by-side with, but looked instead to his own projects. Jefferson did, however, help the government lose its baby-fat by slimming down the military and cutting other unnecessary administrative jobs, lowering taxes and debt at the same time. Nobody fucking does that today. Tom's biggest achievement was "The Louisiana Purchase," when in 1803 he bought a shit ton of land from France for just ten million dollars. This expanded the frontier and gave the United States a few more states to grow into. By 1804, adventurers Meriwether Lewis and William Clark had set out to explore the newly acquired territories and everywhere else they could find in America; they even achieved a feat that was seemingly impossible to most Americans at the time: being fucking nice to the natives.

While Jefferson achieved a lot, the Supreme Court, led by his Federalist cousin John Marshall, still made an effort to give him shit whenever possible. The biggest instance of this was actually helpful to Jefferson in the short run: the 1803 case *Marbury v. Madison* (you had *better* know this one for the test), in which Marshall declared a federal law—that would've actually helped his party out by allowing another Federalist judge to be appointed— to be unconstitutional. The ruling, with a constitutional question being answered by the Supreme

Court, was unprecedented, and with that decision Marshall established the idea of "Judicial Review," asserting that the Supreme Court can determine whether a law is constitutional or not. Marshall wasn't hurt too bad, however, and his court was still stuffed with biased, Federalist judges that Jefferson would consistently squabble with (and even get one of them impeached).

Despite the legal troubles, Tom was re-elected in 1804 by a landslide. Not everyone was happy about it though, and his old VP Aaron Burr (as much of an asshole as he sounds) even tried to convince a bunch of states to secede out of fear that Jefferson had become too Federalist. Burr ended up killing Alexander Hamilton in a duel for indirectly foiling this plot. During his second term, the president not only dealt with these pieces of shit hashing it out, but British efforts to be pieces of shit as well, as evidenced by the *Chesapeake-Leopard* affair, when in 1807 the British warship *Leopard* took a shot at—you guessed it—the American *Chesapeake*. Jefferson reacted to this by pushing the Embargo Act of 1807, which held off the

War of 1812 for another five years by prohibiting all American ships from trading overseas, just because a lot of that trade was with Britain. Petty, but it worked (for a really short amount of time).

TL;DR Thomas Jefferson took the Democratic-Republican ideals he ran on and blended them with the practical measures necessary to keep the Federalists off his ass, but failed still to avoid making enemies and spent his second term dealing with Britain, who was still bitching about the revolution and in turn, fucking with us.

MADISON TRIES TO AVOID THE WAR OF 1812: THE STORY OF WAR OF 1812

After Jefferson came his top pick for a successor, James Madison. Madison was a hard worker who didn't totally fit into the political scene, and thus he was fittingly fucked for the political scene that was about to unfold before him.

Tensions were growing with Britain again, who had been pissy since America became America, and who was subtly fucking with us at every chance they got. Madison tried the Nonintercourse Act of 1809 (Nonintercourse: always lame) that changed Jefferson's really shittily planned embargo to only apply to Britain and France (who was fighting with Britain), as well as Macon's Bill in 1810, which stated that to compensate whichever side agreed to be chill with us first (the kind of recognition a new nation needed) we would cut off all trade with the other. The next year, Napoleon, who wasn't actually that little, but was definitely a little bitch, lied about being chill to get us to piss off the Brits, and then went back to fucking with American ships after promising not to. Merchants in New England were making money off of Napoleon's war, and didn't want to get involved and risk causing peace, but plenty of Democratic-Republicans in the South were had nothing to lose, and were all in for a little attempt at expansionism to clear the bad blood.

Eventually, in 1812 obviously, Madison let the war happen as he rolled into his second term. We tried to invade Canada, and lost every fucking inch we gained. A bunch of people fought in the South and in the water too, gaining nothing but casualties. Andrew Jackson, on the other hand, claimed the national-spotlight as a war hero in the battle of New Orleans in January of 1815 (a month after the Treaty of Ghent was signed to end the war...communication was really goddamn bad at the time). With such little real progress, shit got so tense that some New Englanders even thought about seceding, but after gathering for the Hartford Convention to actually organize it they realized the war was pretty much done. Madison luckily didn't fuck it up even worse by rushing through diplomacy, and he did an overall okay job of showing that the new America could stand its ground against Britain...even if we couldn't invade goddamn Canada correctly.

TL;DR James Madison became president and we went to war with Britain again. It was pretty much for fun. Nobody won but we got to prove we could play with the big dogs.

(1816-1848) AMERICA FINALLY COUNTS AS A REAL COUNTRY: SHIT GETS WEIRD

THE ERA OF GOOD FEELINGS

After James Madison came James Monroe (yeah it's confusing as fuck) in the election of 1816. His presidency marked the start of the "Era of Good Feelings"—i.e. the era after we did okay in a war with Britain so we thought we were the shit. Monroe was another Democratic- Republican who got to watch his opposition pretty much melt away, and while that made it all "good feelings" for people who agreed with him, there were still some silent minorities that were pissed off, and the differences between the North and South were growing more controversial as time went on...

But let's ignore all that subtle shit because that's what any standardized test will do, and instead jump first into the bright colors and the shiny objects over here in the ErA OF GoOd FeELiNgS. Everything nowadays was America!, America!, and America! again, including the tariff of 1816, which passed when America pretended to be so great that it didn't need a good trade relationship with anybody else to help specialize its economy, and Henry Clay's "American System," that pushed for this tariff as well as more spending on national infrastructure projects and a national bank. Soon after this immediate explosion of nationalism came a crash partially caused by the irresponsibility of it all (specifically the shitty national bank), and the Panic of 1819 rushed in a quick recession that really put a damper on the whole "good feelings" aesthetic. Following the panic, Democratic- Republicans split into those who favored a national bank (like the one that caused the recession) and those who stuck to their roots and didn't want one at all. Even John Marshall, still in charge of the court, had to step in again with the case *McCulloch v. Maryland,* in which judicial review was exercised to prove the legitimacy of a national bank in the first place. Monroe balanced these concerns for another term and by the time he was out in 1824, the party was splintering into all sorts of new candidates with a myriad of different ideas. There was one party, sure, but it wasn't unified.

With all the shit going down in America (and insane population growth, partially from immigration, combined with even more insane technological innovations), luckily there was an entire frontier of land for settlers to steal; and steal it they did. Westward expansion became so fervent that Generals Andrew Jackson and William Henry Harrison (both future presidents) were dispatched to push Native-Americans back in advance, and with so much new territory, measures had to be taken to decide how slavery would factor in. Thus began the first step toward the civil war: the Missouri Compromise.

Basically, when Missouri went to become a state, there were already twenty-two: eleven slave states and eleven free. People liked it that way. Neither side had too much power. The only problem was, Missouri was trying to become a state, and there was already slavery there, so admitting it would tip the scales. Rep. James Tallmadge tried to make Missouri a more

balanced state by restricting slavery heavily, and struck out big time with the Tallmadge Amendment in 1820, pissing off and insulting a shit ton of Southerners, showing just how delicate the balance truly was. Shortly after Tallmadge's failure, Congress passed Henry Clay's plan instead, which admitted Missouri as a slave state, admitted Maine as a free state, and used the southern border of Missouri (latitude 360 30') as the line for deciding whether any new state would be slave or free. In other news, we bought Florida from Spain in 1819, and as British relations improved (they even trusted us to fish near canada again). Monroe signed the Monroe Doctrine (you realllly need to know this one) into law, which basically said that if Europeans try to fuck with ANYTHING or ANYONE in the Western Hemisphere, America was ready to drop them. Americans were happy about this nationalistic sentiment, but didn't realize the document would go on to shape America's future fetish for fucking people up/protecting whatever land we decide is all of a sudden our turf.

TL;DR Monroe came after the war and had a pretty easy job, save for some growing sectionalism problems, and everything went back to normal except now Americans pretty much jacked off to the flag.

JACKSON & THE DEMOCRATS

President Andrew Jackson was like anal: you either loved him or you hated him... which is pretty much what you should expect from the guy who became a famous war hero AFTER the peace treaty for that war was signed. He entered the office in 1829, almost exacting vengeance on John Quincy Adams, who he felt stole the last election from him, and that basically set the mood for the rest of his presidency.

Jackson represented the common man of the time. Unfortunately, the common man was not usually a president for a reason, and that reason was that basing decisions off hot-tempered whims gets you into a lot of shitty situations. A few of the major changes under Jackson (which happened often because Jackson saw himself as the judge, jury, and executioner) included suffrage for all white males (kinda progress...I guess?), political favoritism, i.e. Jackson hiring unqualified people because they were loyal to him, using executive order to stop the spread of antislavery literature in the North, and a fuck ton of vetoing, including blocking the recharter bill for the second National Bank, (partially because it was supported by his political enemy, Henry Clay) and a bill to build a road just because it was located in Kentucky, Clay's home state.

Bigger changes came in the Indian Removal Act of 1830, where Jackson responded to the growing expansion westward by forcing tens of thousands of Native-Americans to resettle wherever he damn well pleased. He even took on John Marshall, who declared it illegal for Georgia to push into

Cherokee territory and force the natives out, by, well, pushing into Cherokee territory and forcing the natives out anyway. Marshall wasn't the only guy Jackson pissed off, besides his usual political enemies, Jackson also managed to piss off the entire state of South Carolina when the state wanted to "nullify" a tariff in 1828. The tariff was federal law, a.k.a. Jackson's law, and when the state decided it didn't fit their needs, Jackson

resolved (also like anal) to force it to fit anyway. Jackson pushed Congress to pass a bill that allowed him to use military force in South Carolina, and combined with a slightly lowered tariff, this pressure forced the state to "compromise" with Jackson's will.

Money played a big role as well, in not only Jackson's presidency, but the changing political climate. After Jackson let the Second National Bank fall to pieces, he opened his second term by spreading the federal funds it would have gotten among many smaller banks. He also kinda started the economic Panic of 1837 by doing stuff like this, realizing it caused inflation, and then trying to keep that inflation in check by essentially nullifying paper money. Whigs, who believed in the central bank, would blame Jackson's laissez-faire policies for the depression, and supported those tariffs that Jackson didn't really give a shit about (but pretended to when South Carolina pissed him off). Despite all the things they could blame Jackson for after two terms, his VP, Martin Van Buren, won a third election for the Democrats in 1836. Van Buren unfortunately walked right into the aftermath of Jackson's mess, and took so much shit for the economic recession that his party had lost its dominance by the election of 1840. After Van Buren came William Henry Harrison, a Whig, who died like a month into the job, forcing his VP, John Tyler, to take over for him, who pretty much acted like a Democrat anyway. The trend continues.

TL;DR Andrew Jackson was a rudeass guy who made some iffy decisions, and ended up screwing the economy just enough to knock his party off their high horse by 1840.

RELIGION AND SHIT: THE EARLY 1800s

The rationalist movement (to recap for the cynics, rationalism was basically one long ass episode of *Everybody Hates Christ*) was coming to a close, and at the turn of the 19th century, people were once again waking up to smell the incense; the Second Great Awakening had arrived. From the extremist Puritans to the less go-to-church-or-go-to-hell congregations, everyone was following Jackson's trend of "preaching to the common man" by, well, preaching to the common man. Part of dealing with common men was scaring the shit out of them (this is religion after all), so preachers like Charles G. Finney of New York echoed their predecessor John Edwards of the 1740s (the First Great Awakening), by threatening that if people didn't obey the law of the lord, they'd burn in eternity as soon as they died. That got a lot of people on board.

Preachers would try anything. One guy, William Miller, even told people he knew the exact date Christ would come back for the Rapture, the equivalent of telling kids to be better behaved because Santa is coming soon, and Baptists in the South essentially held campfires to get people to join their church. Mormons did Mormon shit, which was just as weird back then as it is today (if you need an example, Joseph Smith, the Mormons' founder, decided their "holy land" would be in Utah, and that men could have as many wives as they wanted). So bottom line, if you want people to join your religion, offer them extra sex. Of course, all the new ideas for religion were causing little fights between all the new people trying to sell them, and thus the Awakening settled down around the time Andrew Jackson retired.

Culturally, TRANSCENDENTALISM happened. Transcendentalism is the idea of "transcending" material and formal religious shit and moving on to the divinity of nature...it kinda works but isn't exactly perfect if you like being involved in society at all, which the concept demonizes. You'll probably learn about that in English this year, so if I were you

I would find some transcendentalist quote online and memorize it so you can use it on both the English AP and the APUSH exam. The three main brains of Transcendentalism were Ralph Waldo Emerson, a guy who helped start the movement, wrote the book *Self-reliance* to argue for independence from society, and was a huge abolitionist who helped vocalize the antislavery movement before the war, Henry David Thoreau, Emerson's friend who lived in the woods for a couple years to go all-out for the movement, write his famous *Civil Disobedience* essay, and, you know, avoid taxes, and Walt Whitman, who traveled the country to explore sexuality, crowds of people, and write really weird fucking poetry that a lot of people hated on at the time.

Along with the vast movement of Transcendentalism came smaller movements in material arts. The Hudson River School of art focused paintings into natural landscape paintings, authors like Jane Austen pumped out classics like *Pride and Prejudice*, and even architects made a move by adapting Greek columns into American work.

In the family, shit became pretty stereotypical, as men were assigned to making money and women to taking care of the kids, but with a new vigor on both sides, as family sizes shrunk and opinions narrowed. Many women were seen as heroines of the household, idolized for their important and "natural" role, but in the same, some also fought back against societal instructions, from less direct ways (such as simple participation in the abolitionist movement) to more assertive approaches, such as the Seneca Falls Convention of 1848, led by civil rights legend Elizabeth Cady Stanton, which allowed women of all races (and men by the second day, including famous orator, one-time slave, and black abolitionist Frederick Douglass) to air their grievances on the current state but also to plan for change. The results would eventually come not only in their abolitionist efforts, but also in their push for women's suffrage, which would be achieved through the 19th amendment during the 20th century.

TL;DR In pre 1850 culture, nobody agreed. Women made some moves to be less housewife-y…and other women wanted to be even more housewife-y. Artists tried out new things while authors denounced materialism, and these same denouncers of materialism were pissed off by the huge new growth of religious activists, who were pissing each other off by not agreeing on anything.

POLITICAL MOVEMENTS: THE OTHER STUFF FROM THE EARLY 1800s

Along with all the religious and cultural clashes of the early 19th century came political fights lacking none of the tension.

What's the easiest way to piss people off politically? Try to take away their alcohol. That's what the "temperance" movement did, by basically claiming that all the bad things in America were due to drinking, and therefore banning drinking would solve all those problems. Some states got on board, and a bunch of middle classers too, but immigrants who wanted to grab a bottle were gonna grab a bottle, regardless of what a few religious leaders from far-far-away thought. On a positive note came a public push for more public goods. Leaders like Dorothea Dix fought for mental hospitals, State governments worked on changing how prisons worked (but seriously fucking up a lot of people in their creepy experiments), early versions of poor housing were established, and schools were finally built specifically for the blind and deaf. Even "free" public schooling was beginning to grow…though often educating creepily with textbooks that supported temperance and the Second Great Awakening. Religious colleges began the trend of universities, which would pop up in the era as well, changing the face of education as people came back from the Civil War years later. As we head into sectionalism in the next chapters, note that abolitionist movements were starting to spring up, as evidenced in William Lloyd Garrison's specifically abolitionist newspaper, *The Liberator*, and his subsequent founding of the American Antislavery Society. Change was coming, and everyone knew it.

TL;DR Politics started to grow and clash. The people called for more public goods and the government provided, but all of this positive change was to some degree just papering over the cracks of slavery and temperance.

NEW TERRITORY: PEOPLE ARE MOVING, SHIT HAPPENS

As people moved west into the expanding frontier (thanks to Jefferson's Louisiana purchase) major changes were bound to arise. The North and South, for one, kept arguing about slavery, so every time a new territory looked to become a state, shit got expectedly heated. This led to stuff like the Missouri Compromise, one of Monroe's achievements, that basically aimed to keep things balanced between the cotton-lovin, tariff hatin', racist-ass southern assholes and the godly, perfect, industrial and generally abolitionist Northerners (can you guess where the authors are from?).

Innovations were also born to help transport an exponentially growing population off to the newly acquired lands, including steamboats, the construction of the Erie Canal (for those steamboats to use), and a shit ton of railroads popping up. Patent laws protected new inventions and helped incentivize more of them. Unions protected (well, tried and mostly failed to) the workers operating them. Agriculture skyrocketed in the South due to all the cheap land, and with Eli Whitney's cotton gin, that helped separate usable cotton from its seeds, the cash-crop of the time became even more pervasive. Slavery too grew as an institution, but the number of slaves compared to the number of other workers actually shrank, as poor white farmers saw these new technologies alienating them further from the rich slave owners they hoped to become.

As the North and South innovated and expanded their differences, there was still plenty of conflict left for the frontier. Mountain men carved the Oregon trail while setting up a fair share of hick towns along the way. Women had more freedom on the frontier, able to work as doctors or assistants on farms if they wanted. Settlers basically fucked up half the forests they crossed paths with by not giving a shit about the environment. Native-Americans, physically forced out by Jackson in his early years and politically forced out during his presidency, adapted to nomadic ways of life, using horses traded to them by the Spanish immigrants of Mexico.

Speaking of Mexico...we kinda went to war with them. A lot of American nationalists were high on the idea of "Manifest Destiny," a concept writer John D. Sullivan pulled out of his ass, which stated basically that it was America's responsibility to stretch from sea to shining sea (and fuck up anyone who got in her way). So of course, when Mexico offered Americans free money to move out west and settle what would become Texas, people jumped at the opportunity. Of course, after everyone got there, Americans literally crossed the line by assuming their border would be the Rio Grande and inching right up to it. The Mexican government didn't approve, so the Americans ignored their laws and pissed them off until the Mexicans became just aggressive enough to be blamed for starting the war. It helped that massive expansionist dickhead James K. Polk had been elected in 1844. Things got tense in the mini-war, and in 1848, just after the Alamo (remember it?) the Mexican general was captured and forced to sign the Treaty of Guadalupe Hidalgo, giving up the territories of Texas (duh), Arizona, California, Utah, Nevada, Colorado, Wyoming (yeah, it's real) and, obviously, New Mexico. America had continued to push the bounds elsewhere, pissing off the Brits in Oregon and the Canadians (which were really the Brits again) in Maine, but none escalated to such fucked-up levels as the Mexican-American War.

TL;DR As technology grew, so did the amount of bitching from the South about the North fighting slavery. Also the U.S. fucked up Mexico, pretended that Mexico started it, and stole the land the Mexico had just stolen from the natives.

(1848-1863) THE CIVIL WAR: BECAUSE AMERICA WILL KICK ITS OWN ASS IF IT NEEDS TO

CIVIL WAR POLITICS: AMERICA PLAYS WITH ITSELF

Typically, on standardized testing at least, what happens in a war is actually not that important, and if you can figure out how to work a significant battle into an essay then you probably already know your shit, so no need to cover it again. This book is designed for those who either don't know their shit or don't want to know the shit they don't need to know. Thus, this chapter will touch on the events of the Civil War itself less and will focus instead on the causes of it.

In summary, the Civil War was a fight between the South and the North that was about slavery, but not as much about slavery as most people think. There was also tension between the two regions because of tariffs that hurt the South while helping the North, other economic disparities, differing opinions over how much power a state should have (versus the federal government), and in Lincoln's opinion at least, not allowing the Union to fall apart.

The election of 1848, in which Whig candidate Zachary Taylor (a General in the Mexican-American War) took office, set things into motion. As new states looked to enter America, Taylor was awkwardly positioned as a slaveholder, who had to balance the needs of other states and new territories when deciding who to admit and under what conditions. At the same time, a growing "free soil" movement (spearheaded by Northern Democrats and many in Taylor's own party) was taking root, which argued that argued any lands won from Mexico should be slave free...which sounds great until one realizes that it wouldn't be just slaves barred from living in the territory, but all blacks. Yeah, we were that fucked up.

The first plight for Taylor was California, a territory that—though split by that line the Missouri-Compromise had drawn up—was determined to enter the union as a free-state. Taylor said "fuck it, let's let you guys in immediately and throw in

New Mexico as a free state too." This move monumentally pissed off Southerners, who would've fucked shit up right then and there if Henry Clay, a career beta-male politician, known for trying really hard to be president and never succeeding, hadn't stepped in.

Clay suggested a compromise on three main points: Let in Cali as a free state, split New Mexico into two states (New Mexico and Utah), and let them decide for themselves whether to be slave states or free states (this idea is called "Popular Sovereignty" and is VERY important to understand. Remember it.), and create a vigilantly followed new Fugitive Slave Law to keep those Southerners happy. The Senate and Clay engaged in a heated debate over what the hell they were gonna do, and finally agreed to the "Compromise of 1850." By the time this agreement had been made, Taylor had died (don't worry about it, it just happened), and his VP Millard Fillmore filled in (pun very intended), supporting the compromise and helping to pass each piece of it through Congress. Extremists on both sides weren't happy, but enough people were semi-satisfied to hold back the shitstorm of the Civil War for another few years. The compromise also ended up giving the North a bit more political strength as slave-free territories started creeping into the South. In response to these new regulations, the resistance changed too, Harriet Tubman and the Underground Railroad, a messy slave- escape route that helped many southern Blacks reach northern freedom, was forced to push further, reaching either to Canada or sections of the country where the Fugitive Slave Law was not enforced by pissed off anti-slavery Northerners. Cultural support, such as the the famous novel *Uncle Tom's Cabin* by Harriet Beecher Stowe, which detailed the plights of a fictional slave living in the South, also erupted from the base of Northern abolitionists, who tolerated the compromise without truly supporting it. In the South, slavery-supporters would go as far as claiming that masters were like fathers to their slaves, and that as an institution slavery provided a twisted "beauty" that the northern industrialists could not achieve. Even new political parties emerged of the flooding controversy, notably the Know Nothing Party, who supported nationalism and were anti-immigration but did pretty much nothing else, and the Republicans, who at the time were at the hub of abolitionist thought and action.

Two years into the compromise it was election time again, with Franklin Pierce taking office for the Democrats in 1852, beating the poor Whigs in a landslide, who had just seen their last candidate serve half a term before eating it. Pierce was a moderate pick, who was born in the North but supported the compromise just enough to get southern support and northern tolerance. Now that the Democrats had prerogative, the northern roots were not enough to keep the Pierce administration in check, and Senator Stephen A. Douglass really messed with shit when he proposed the Kansas-Nebraska Act in 1854, to garner Southern support for his new Transcontinental Railroad idea, that allowed the territories of Kansas and Nebraska to enter the Union under popular sovereignty, which gave the South an opportunity to get back at the North for encroaching on Southern space by risking the introduction of slavery to Northern territory (all this really just ignored the Missouri Compromise). The Act was passed, hesitantly, and the Republicans in the North were universally pissed off. So were many racist people, as always, and fighting erupted between the settlers who planned to vote "free-state" and those who planned to vote "slave-state" just a year into the Act. This fuckuppery was officially known as "Bleeding Kansas," with both sides brutally murdering each other. John Brown, an antislavery father, brought his kids to help literally hack people to death at an opposing farm settlement. Shit was getting real. Pierce didn't intervene.

Republicans channeled this anger into a strong 1856 campaign, but still lost to the Democrats, who swapped the pointless Franklin Pierce for James Buchanan. Buchanan would serve until 1861 and see a bunch of shit happen that he didn't really have much say in. First, some settlers in Kansas tried to become a slave-state by proposing their Lecompton Constitution, which Buchanan was cool with, but Congress said no because the vast majority of Kansas was *not* cool with it. Kansas ended up becoming a free state. Along with this controversy came the 1857 *Dred Scott v. Sanford* Case, in which a slave (Dred Scott) who had traveled with his master to a free state was denied freedom by the courts, AND the Supreme Court had the nerve to add that Dred Scott shouldn't have even be allowed to sue his master as he was not a citizen. The North was—understandably—pissed the fuck off, and tensions only grew with a newly elected Democrat in office. Lincoln also showed his face in major politics by running against Stephen Douglas (and losing) for an Illinois senate seat, though Lincoln impressed many with his oratory skills and sharp mind during the debates. Other Republicans were winning Congressional seats, however, and the prospect of Republican rule and the economic shitstorm for the South that came with it (higher tariffs and less slavery), scared the hell out of a lot of Southern Whites. What scared them even more was the return of John Brown, the abolitionist who killed a bunch of guys for some family-friendly fun during Bleeding Kansas. Brown and his family started a slave uprising in 1859 known as the "Raid on Harpers Ferry," that took two days for the Virginia government (and eventually federal troops) to shut down. When Brown was finally captured, him and his co conspirators were hanged.

The straw that broke the camel's back was the 1860 election, where split Democrats couldn't agree on a candidate pragmatic enough to take down Lincoln. South Carolina, probably still pissy about the nullification crisis under Jackson, seceded first from the Union in December (Before Lincoln even got in office), and was followed swiftly by Alabama, Florida, Georgia, Louisiana, Mississippi, and Texas. The newly formed Confederate States of America did pretty much exactly what anyone would expect, and made a new constitution that restricted their government's power to restrict slavery or to promote tariffs. The South wasn't planning on budging. Neither was Lincoln, thus...war.

The war began with a diplomatic struggle, which is why many

southern states still call the Civil War "The War of Northern Aggression" (seriously, confirmed by a friend from Florida). In 1861, the North-controlled Fort Sumter off the coast of South Carolina was dangerously low on supplies. When Lincoln wanted to send a boat of food and other non- military needs, the South declared that they would fight back against this..."aggression." Lincoln wasn't having this shit and sent the boat in anyway, fighting ensued and the battery of Fort Sumter is considered the first—but definitely not the worst—of the fucking up the Civil War would bring. For the next four years the Union and Confederates would go at it, the Union finally winning by their superior manufacturing ability and greater numbers. The Union took the aggressive, necessary steps to win, strategically splitting the South by taking the Mississippi River and using droves of new technology to do so, including some of the first ships with iron siding. Lincoln got a little bit of politics into his term (and second term that was cut short by assassination) through two major introductions: The Emancipation Proclamation of 1862, that freed slaves in all states the Union was fighting (there were actually some border states that stayed in the Union but still allowed slavery during the war), and the Thirteenth Amendment to the Constitution, which ended slavery once and for all. Lincoln was also lowkey a bitch that didn't really care about the slaves (just about holding the Union together) and did some shady ass shit like suspending Habeas Corpus (the writ that says you have to be told why you are in jail if you are arrested), but he got the job done and was too busy dying for anyone to call him out on his bullshit. We found you out, "Honest Abe."

TL;DR The Civil War, between the antislavery North and the proslavery South, was also about tariffs, expansionism, states' rights, and sometimes personal beefs. The North obviously won, and the Republican party was created not only to manifest Northern sentiments into a political body, but became super powerful for the next century as well.

(1863-1877) RECONSTRUCTION AFTER THE CIVIL WAR: TIME TO CLEAN UP THE MESS

RECONSTRUCTION

Typically, after you fuck yourself up in a civil war, whoever wins is first tasked with stacks and stacks of unfuckery-work to be done. Before the war was won (and Lincoln got his head blown off), Abe put together a plan to reintegrate southern states by a small test of loyalty. The president issued in 1863 a Proclamation of Amnesty and Reconstruction, which let southern states come back if they accepted that slavery was done and took an oath of allegiance to the the Union (only ten percent had to agree to this, so Lincoln was pretty much ready to let in the ninety percent who wanted to blow his head off scot free). Most Republicans realized the "ninety-percent-of-these-guys-wanna-kill-me" problem and responded with a counterplan, the Wade-Davis Bill of 1864. This Bill required that fifty percent of Southerners took the new oath (the "only-half-these-guys-wanna-kill-me" compromise), and took away some voting rights for confederates. Lincoln did a "pocket-veto" on this bill, which means he never actually vetoed it, he just didn't even sign it at all to be extra fucking petty, so it technically couldn't become law.

After Lincoln died, President Andrew Johnson, the Southerner Lincoln chose as his Vice President to keep things balanced, issued a similar plan to Lincoln's, but maintained a little more power in the oval office for pardons, which he ended up using a lot anyway (allowing a bunch of confederate asshats to take office again just a few years after the war). Another of the Johnson administration changes was the Freedmen's Bureau, created by Congress in 1865. It basically helped out both poor Blacks and Whites. It was supposed to help them find homes in confiscated southern land, but this plan got kinda fucked when the Bureau realized Johnson gave most of this land back to the original, Confederate owners. One thing the Bureau didn't fuck up was education, however, and it established thousands of schools for free Blacks, the first effort to curb illiteracy in freed slaves.

Just as predicted by the Republicans, there were still many racist southern assholes running around doing what assholes do. Many southern states implemented "Black Codes" that restricted African-Americans heavily, sometimes even forcing them to sign work contracts that paralleled slavery. Johnson pissed off more Republicans by vetoing a bill to help the Freedmen's Bureau, one of the few successes of his tenure, and a civil rights bill meant to take down the Black Codes. The president was elected again (but really for the first time) in 1866, but his second term started with immediate Congressional efforts to overturn those vetoes, instating the Civil Rights Act of 1866 that declared all African-Americans to be citizens, which was later backed up by the Fourteenth Amendment, solidifying that anyone born in the U.S. was therefore a citizen and must be treated as such by their state government. It also fucked up Johnson's earlier changes by demanding that Confederates could no longer hold office.

The Republicans weren't done beating the living shit out of Johnson though. They hit him once again with the Reconstruction Acts of 1867, that passed over his vetoes, giving the Union army prerogative over the newly reintegrated southern states and forcing them to ratify the fourteenth amendment. Then, they passed the Tenure of Office Act that forbade Johnson from firing people, so when he finally did in 1868, they could (and would) impeach him. Johnson was one vote away from being kicked out of office. That same year was another election year and, obviously, Johnson didn't get elected.

Instead, Ulysses S. Grant, a war hero who didn't know shit about politics, was elected for the Republicans to continue with stage two of unfuckery. Grant won because of the Black vote for the liberal Republican party, and with this precedent his administration continued advancing Black rights, through the Fifteenth Amendment that secured the vote for all citizens and the Civil Rights Act of 1875, which guaranteed equal treatment by public businesses (like railroads). Reconstruction came with corruption, often from Grant's friends; he was surrounded by greedy cabinet members that took advantage of the low attention to economic regulation. A big example of this is the Credit Mobilier affair, in which Congressmen were paid off by businesses with stock to ignore the huge profits bosses were raking in.

Grant got re-elected anyway 'cause people still hated the southern Democrats. At the start of term two, Grant's lack of focus on structuring the economy came back to bite him in the ass when the Panic of 1873 ensued, following major overspending from Reconstruction era inflation. Reconstruction in turn became a more moderate process. An Amnesty Act was passed in 1872 that brought Southerners back to the table for holding office and engaging in politics, and five years later a new president, Rutherford B. Hayes, ended the Union military's babysitting of the South with the Compromise of 1877. The compromise also funded a transcontinental railroad in the South for brownie points.

TL;DR Lincoln made a plan that Congress didn't like, after Lincoln got merc'd Johnson did that plan and a bunch of other shit Congress didn't like. Later Grant came in who did a good job with Reconstruction and a pretty shitty job with everything else. Finally Hayes ended Reconstruction officially...that's pretty much all he did.

(1877-1900) GILDED AGE POLITICS: HOW TO BULLY PEOPLE AND GENTRIFY THEM AT THE SAME TIME

THE POLITICAL SHIT AFTER RECONSTRUCTION

"Gilded Age" politics was just a series of boring ass presidents, some of which were also boring asshole presidents. Nobody really took any strong position on most issues because the generally accepted move was to not piss people off as much as everybody had been pissed off for the first three quarters of the nineteenth century. President Rutherford B. Hayes let shit do what shit did and didn't get involved, but his semi-significance comes from showing support for the growing temperance (no alcohol) movement and ending Reconstruction when he was first elected. He tried to veto the Bland-Allison Act, which favored Nevada miners by allowing silver coins to be minted in limited supply, but the Act was passed over his veto. James Garfield came next, winning by a close vote for the Republicans, and got merc'd soon after by a political enemy. His VP, Chester A. Arthur, stepped up and impressed people in his one term by building up the Navy and working against this huge ass tariff the Republicans liked, so he took some shit for that but otherwise was kinda done with politics afterwards.

Grover Cleveland, actually a pretty good guy for the time, came next as the first Democrat in a while to take office. He stuck to small government but used it to cut corruption, like hunting down the dickheads who pretended to be Civil War Veterans for pension money, and signed onto the big bills from the time like the Interstate Commerce Act. Cleveland echoed Arthur in challenging the high tariffs of the Republicans. He also echoed his predecessor by taking major shit from the Republicans because of it.

As the century began to close and Cleveland finished his first term, people generally didn't care about politics. The tariffs that kept coming up revived excitement because people actually had to take a side: Cleveland and the Democrats wanted a lower tariff because it raised prices for consumers and counter tariffs were fucking over the already fucked southern farmers, Republicans and their 1888 winning candidate, Benjamin Harrison, liked higher tariffs because they boosted businesses in the North by removing their international competition.

With people giving a shit once again and the Republicans in Congress and the White House, shit got done. The McKinley Tariff was passed in 1890, taxing foreign imports at almost 50%, veteran pensions were handed out like free samples, and the Sherman Antitrust Act finally took the first step towards ending the systematic fucking over of the poor you'll read about in a couple pages.

The Populist party rose to center stage as politics became something for the populus again. They formed an ambitious "Omaha" platform that consisted of trying to get more silver money, a progressive income tax, and basically a bunch of other shit to help out the less fortunate, including early labor laws. In the 1892 election, the Populists didn't win, but their presence showed the growth of renewed engagement by Americans. Cleveland came back and clinched the victory over Harrison in his redemption fight. Unfortunately for Cleveland, as soon as he won the presidency the American economy entered the shitstorm that would become of the Panic of 1893, following all the over excitement of the Industrial Revolution. Cleveland actually had to get a bail out from J.P. Morgan, which goes to show how interconnected business and politics were at the time. In 1896, the election was way more heated than it had been for years, as populist William Jennings Bryan stole the Democratic nomination from Cleveland in an upset after delivering his harrowing "Cross of Gold" speech, in which he argued that Cleveland's support for the gold standard over silver money was basically the same thing as crucifying America. Idk man.

Bryan lost the real election—obviously—he was just a screaming lunatic who only got nominated because he inspired a few people for thirty-five minutes on a Thursday afternoon. The new president, William McKinley, was a tariff man who successfully blamed the Democrats for causing the panic of 1893 (which started right after the Republicans had complete political control four years). His presidency marked a domestic political shift from rural populism to urban republicanism, and he passed another tariff to keep things consistent. Most of his focus was international in the Spanish-American war, but you'll read about that shortly.

Finally, another important political note to make is the 1896 supreme court case of *Plessy v. Ferguson*, which dictated that segregation was okay, along with the Jim Crow laws that enforced it. This was just one hint of the larger problem of institutional racism that had grown from the moment slaves were freed some thirty years before.

TL;DR After Hayes, people didn't really give two shits about the government and the government didn't really give one shit back, but energy went back to normal when Democrats started hating on insane tariff and Republicans in turn bitched about that hatred.

THE CULTURAL SHIT AFTER RECONSTRUCTION

As America was rebuilding itself in a whole new world, its culture too was struggling to grow into an alien environment.

In the South, racism was as permeating as economic troubles. Much of early Post- Reconstruction was still basically Reconstruction for them, as impoverished farmers tried everything from rehiring freed slaves as "sharecroppers," (an institution almost as inescapable as slavery) to diversifying their crops past cotton into other warm weather plants, such as soybeans and sweet potatoes. Many even joined unions of their own, such as the Farmers' Southern Alliance and the segregated Colored Farmers' National Alliance. As the North pulled out (lol) presence from the South in the 1870s, more and more tricks were used by the racist White dicks in power to keep Black citizens out of the polls, including poll taxes, literacy tests, and segregated primaries. Many African-American citizens were not considered for job titles Whites felt were "too good" for them and were not allowed to serve on juries...essentially a lot of racist idiots fucked themselves over while trying to fuck over people they hated, fucking everything over in the long run.

With all this troublesome fuckery in the South, northern cities only had more people willing to immigrate to their growing hubs of culture. Immigrants flocked to the North East, flushing cities like New York, Boston and Philadelphia with quick change and bustling cultures. The U.S. population actually tripled from the Civil War to turn of the century. There was even conflict between different types of immigrants, it was no longer just "fuck you I was born here,"(Americans to everyone) but "fuck you I came here ten years ago"(Western European immigrants to Mediterranean ones). The Chinese Exclusion Act, which forbade any immigration from China, was passed in 1882, and became the first in a long list of toughening requirements for new immigrants seeking entrance into America.

As the cities filled with men, they filled with man-made marvels as well. Skyscrapers replaced smaller buildings, horse-drawn streetcars replaced walking, and were soon replaced by railways and subways. Ethnic neighborhoods preserved old cultures in new cities, and gentrified suburbs grew to surround those cities. People contracted a fuck-ton of new and exciting diseases in the grimey conditions of these cities.

With change comes cynics, and in the late 1800s there were plenty. Henry George gave industrial giants shit with his social commentary *Progress and Poverty*, whereas Edward Bellamy drew up a trouble-free world where everyone gave a shit in his utopian guidebook *Looking Backward, 2000-1887*.

Religious people also got to say their peace when some high-up Protestant guys started the idea of a "Social Gospel," claiming that middle class should work to apply Christian goodwill to solving problems faced by the city-slickers of the day. Religion grew big time as many immigrants brought theirs with them, especially Catholics, boosting memberships to church based organizations as well. Divorce rates ironically rose, and more steps were taken for the empowerment of women along those lines, such as the birth of the National American Woman Suffrage Association under iconic orator Elizabeth Cady Stanton.

Public schools and colleges sprung up, the study of evolution was taken more seriously and people in the social sciences got pissed off at the government. America was looking more modern everyday.

Even art became important, as musicians like Jelly Roll Morton showed us early forms of Jazz or Louis Sullivan brought architecture to its grassy-roots in the cold gray city of Chicago. Mark Twain did his thing and published *The Adventures of Huckleberry Finn* in 1884. Abstract paintings became a thing. People weren't afraid to relax and watch sports or invent them, and having leisure-time no longer meant you were irresponsible. Life started out pretty shittily after Reconstruction, but America made the best of it.

TL;DR Reconstruction's end was followed by Southern hatred, which led to Northern city migration, which came with a whole new slew of things: immigration, innovation, sports, art, social criticism, and a new culture of the overworked that appreciated relaxation.

THE NATIVE PEOPLE (AND FARMERS) ARE FUCKED YET AGAIN

Another change that must be noted in the later 1800s is all the shit that went down with farmers, the frontier, and the freedmen.

In 1893, Frederick Jackson Turner wrote his essay "The Significance of the Frontier on American History," claiming that the door of new American land to conquer was now...closed. He argued that the absence of expansion would cause a fuck ton of new problems, because we no longer had our favorite backup plan for pissing people off: running away.

He was right as fuck.

In the late 1800s, the U.S. started a really messy process of removing Native- Americans, which involved reigniting Andrew Jackson's reservation policy (that majorly butted heads with the natives' "We-will-migrate-where-we-damn-well-please" policy), resulting in a series of "Indian Wars" with the native plains people at the edge of the dying frontier. All this eventuated in the Dawes Severalty of 1887, which broke down tribes by dividing their land into plots for individual families to tend. This plan got fucked up when a lot of the land meant for the natives ended up in the hands of White settlers anyway. Tensions were finally flushed by the natives' last stand in the massacre of Wounded Knee, in which Sioux tribesmen were shot to pieces by invading Whites because a gun was accidentally fired while being confiscated by the invaders. These broken people would go unaided until FDR finally stepped in over forty years later.

Farmers had it much better than the Natives, but all in all their lives were still going pretty shittily. Southern farmers were already moderately fucked when the North destroyed a bunch of their livestock and farmland during the war, but as prices for crops fell, especially for cotton, their incomes and standards of living became even worse. The National Grange Movement, led by Oliver H. Kelley, sprung up in response to this sweeping issue, even passing laws regulating railroads needed for transporting agricultural products (these state regulations on public businesses were held up in the Supreme Court Case *Munn v. Illinois* in 1877). The farmers got slightly fucked when the Supreme Court ruled in *Wabash v. Illinois* that a state government couldn't regulate interstate commerce, but Congress made up for this with the Interstate Commerce Act of 1886, that set up a federal agency to make sure railroads weren't jacking up prices to jack off their profit margins.

As Reconstruction ended in 1877, Black Southerners were the hardest hit, as the only thing more racist than post-slavery White Southerners is impoverished post-slavery White Southerners. Though federal law dictated equal treatment, the ex-Confederates took some liberty to take away some liberties, often ignoring the new amendments they had signed onto. This came in the form of locally enforced Black Codes (which later morphed into Jim Crow laws), the civil rights case *Plessy v. Ferguson*, which determined that separate but "equal" facilities counted as equal treatment, and the *Civil Rights Cases* of 1883, which struck down most of the antiracism progress made under the Congresses of Reconstruction. Sometimes

White men would even wait outside polling booths with guns to scare away Black voters.

Leaders like Booker T. Washington, a former slave who advocated for African-Americans to free themselves by education, or W.E.B. Du Bois, who called for a swift and drastic end to segregation, showed that with freedom from slavery came at least a representative voice for African-Americans, if not, ya know, any real change in the first 50 years of freedom.

TL;DR Native-Americans got fucked by the government and fought back. Same thing with farmers. Same thing with African-Americans.

RICH PEOPLE AREN'T FUCKED (YET AGAIN)

From 1860 to 1900, while immigrants of all kinds were discriminated against, farmers suffered, natives suffered, and former slaves suffered, the people who were not suffering were —you guessed it—really fucking rich people.

This time period, often referred to as "The Industrial Revolution" was really great for rich people because their preferred method of getting rich (abusing poor people) was very legal and by far the easiest way to achieve their goals.

Railroads are a key example of how the "Laissez-Faire" (French for "stay the fuck out of it") economy helped consumers and hurt the labor force. It all started when tycoon Cornelius Vanderbilt decided to create a system of national rail lines all using the same gauges (track size) so his trains could get to wherever he wanted. This revolutionized rail travel (and transport of goods over rails), earning him a virtual monopoly over the industry. The government fucked things up by giving out land and money to anyone building railroads, which encouraged plenty of shitty people to build plenty of shitty railroads that were barely relevant when compared to empires like Vanderbilt's. What's more is that Vanderbilt's real competition was few and far between, and the collection of giants controlling the rail industry weren't afraid to jack up prices and hold down wages. In 1877, rail workers across America got so pissed about being hit with a pay cut that they held a gigantic, violent strike against their employers. Hayes had to sent in troops to stop it.

Workers in all industries—from Andrew Carnegie's steel empire to John D. Rockefeller's Standard Oil Trust—got pissed about their conditions, but with the huge amount of available immigrants to replace them and next to zero economic regulations, there wasn't really much they could do. Some tried to join unions, such as the National Labor Union or Knights of Labor (bonus points to Terence V. Powderly for including African-Americans and women in his group, minus some points for the goofy ass name), but with events like the rail strike, and again, no laws protecting labor, it was easy for employers just to fire at will. Popular moves included: yellow-dog contracts (you can't work for me unless you promise not to join a union), blacklists ("hey this guy's in a union don't hire him"), and even just hiring a whole fucking mercenary army to break up a strike. It happened. Shit continued to get real throughout the end of the century, as sampled in events such as the Haymarket bombing, when several police officers were killed by an anarchist and the Knights of Labor were blamed for it because they were close by, and in the Pullman strike, when union leader Eugene Debs was sent to jail to break a strike that pretty much just involved rail workers fucking up their bosses' rail cars a little bit. Henry Clay Frick, who managed one of Carnegie's steel plants, really got a taste for fucking with the poor when he cut his workers' wages down by a fifth of what they had been, realized this would cause a strike, and closed the factory down for a little while afterwards (hiring armed guards to protect it) so people wouldn't have anywhere at which to actually to host their strike. Brutal.

For all the bad of this time period, there was some good. Immigration and urbanization accompanied the rise of towering skyscrapers and suburbs to surround them. The era was characterized by innovation, from Cyrus Field's

Transatlantic cable at its beginnings to the early escalator and jukebox at the end. Edison did his thing. Lightbulbs were a thing now. So was public schooling. David Ricardo wrote about his thing, specialization, and more and more companies began to employ his ideas for systems of maximal efficiency, producing a shit ton more shit. As more and more stuff was available for purchase, with new railroads allowing this stuff to be transported across the country, the people selling it raked in tons of cash. Many people had the opportunity to join a growing middle class in working management for these tycoons, though many more were left behind in the dust of poverty. Luckily, the impoverished at least had a little hope inspired through reading novels like *Ragged Dick* (lol) by Horatio Alger Jr., which detailed rags-to-riches stories that were rare as fuck in real life but still nice to daydream about.

TL;DR During the Industrial Revolution, a lack of economic boundaries/ regulations allowed industries to be...revolutionized, but this revolution came at a price. Luckily for rich people, that price was just fucking over their employees, a policy they made liberal use of. Employees fought back, but found very little success.

(1867-1900) INTERVENTION: AMERICA PUTS ITS DICK IN A BUNCH OF PEOPLE'S FACES

AMERICA GETS TIRED OF ITSELF: IMPERIALISM BEGINS

Realizing after the Civil War that internal conflict sucks, America decided to no longer sit alone in the corner of the global sandbox touching itself. In the gap between the Civil War and World War One, the U.S. expanded both its territories and international friendships.

William H. Seward, Secretary of State under Abe Lincoln and Andrew Johnson, started this trend by annexing Midway Island in the Pacific and building a canal in Nicaragua. Napoleon III, who was just as much a backstabbing bitch as his uncle Napoleon I, moved his troops into Mexico while the US was distracted by the Civil War. Luckily for the U.S.,

Napoleon III wasn't just a backstabbing bitch, he was a regular bitch too, and he ran away as soon as Seward threatened to use the Monroe Doctrine to kick him out in 1865. Also thanks to Seward, the U.S. Congress purchased Alaska in 1867. Nobody actually thanked Seward though, because he basically convinced us to buy a gigantic, icy wasteland.

Forgetting its entire history of struggling for independence, the United States furthered its quest to force weaker nations to struggle to keep their independence. The influences to do this came from everywhere. For one, many other powerful countries were also taking over the world, and the U.S. didn't want to get left behind. Missionaries encouraged the U.S. to expand so they could spread Christianity in the usual way: military force and racism. Republican Congressmen like Henry Cabot Lodge and Teddy Roosevelt also supported expansionism, hoping to find new trade opportunities for the businessmen that had voted them into office. Even the people in journalism wanted expansion so they'd have more interesting things to write about. The government responded to this call by heavily increasing its Naval strength and setting course to anywhere it could conquer (typically countries that were poor, nearby, or indefensible islands).

TL;DR When the Civil War ended, the United States stopped looking at itself and started focusing on everybody else. Expansionism was triggered by the work of Secretary of State William H. Seward, and was continued by missionaries, Congressmen, businessmen, and the government officials trying to get all these peoples' votes.

AMERICA STARTS WITH LATIN AMERICA

Now that the United States was absorbing its enemies, it also wanted to focus on keeping its friends. This took root in the work of James G. Blaine, the Secretary of State under Benjamin Harrison. Blaine set up the Pan-American Conference in 1889, where a bunch of countries from the Western Hemisphere met to talk about economic and political problems. The Conference would grow into an organization that helped those established friendships grow and stay healthy.

A few years later, when Grover Cleveland noticed a border dispute between Venezuela and a British Colony, he whipped out the Monroe Doctrine, pressuring Great Britain to arbitrate the dispute instead of letting it germinate into a full-fledged war.

Obviously, Britain's arbitration determined that Britain was right, and America's attempt at "intervention" really just cucked Venezuela out of any chance at victory. Despite the fact that the U.S. really didn't do shit, Latin America was actually grateful that America almost attempted to try. We were making friends.

TL;DR The U.S. made friends with Latin American countries in the late 1800s by talking to them a lot and helping them a little.

THE SPANISH-AMERICAN WAR

President McKinley didn't believe in interventionism, but he was a politician, so he did believe in being easily peer pressured. In the 1890s the United States was plunged into the Spanish-American war despite better judgement, thanks to a smirkus-board of factors. In 1895, Cuban revolutionaries started destroying plantations, many of which America had invested in, as a strategy to defeat their Spanish rulers economically. Journalists were encouraging war once again by exaggerating to make more money (this is called "Yellow Journalism"), which was very easy to do because there was plenty of drama to report on, such as the De Lôme letter, a message from Spanish minister Dupuy de Lôme that criticized the president, and the sinking of the *Maine,* an American ship that was likely sunk by an accidental explosion but was blamed on the Spanish.

McKinley demanded in 1898 that Spain agree to a ceasefire in Cuba. Other people in America wanted to fight Spain,

—

however, so McKinley gave in and asked Congress to declare war. Obviously Congress agreed because they were also elected by the people calling for war. Solidifying the notion that this war was really just America squashing beef with Spain, Congress created the Teller Amendment, which declared that the United States was going to liberate Cuba and then leave it alone, instead of trying to take it over as a colony.

The war itself was short as hell, and took place entirely in the spring and summer of 1898. Spain was fucked. The United States quickly took Cuba with an army of volunteers that

were more likely to die from the tropical diseases than to be casualties of war. The fight in Cuba ended when Teddy Roosevelt's "Rough Riders" took San Juan Hill in July. Meanwhile, the United States also took over the Philippines from Spain for shits and giggles, officially ending the war when Manila was captured in August.

TL;DR The president didn't want to go to war with Spain, which was kinda breaking the Monroe Doctrine in Cuba. Everybody else did want to though, so McKinley gave up and the U.S. easily won and started conquering shit on the side.

The 1900s: Now America is Actually Important

PEACE BE WITH U.S.

As peace came and a treaty needed to be signed, things were
looking more shitty than during the war. Part of the treaty was
giving Cuba independence, something everybody knew would
happen and therefore no one gave a fuck about. The rest,
however, was just America taking other people's shit... the
treaty added that in order to have peace Spain must give the
U.S. Guam, Puerto Rico, and the Philippines. People didn't
like the Philippines part because it was basically violating
everything America was supposed to believe in. The
government didn't care, and took Philippines, which tried to
revolt, but was crushed as the American military spent three
years systematically destroying their revolution—right after
the same military assisted another countries revolutionaries in
overthrowing their oppressive imperialist rulers. Ironic, huh.

The American people were mad about all the shit going on that
they never signed up for, but the economy was doing well, so
they ignored all the injustice and military cruelty and re-
elected McKinley in 1900 with Theodore Roosevelt as his VP.

Though the U.S. had promised to immediately leave Cuba after
helping it win the war...it didn't. By 1901, America was getting
bored of the occupation and agreed to leave Cuba for real this
time on the condition that Cuba always let the U.S. have power
over its foreign policy, through the Platt Amendment. Cuba
angrily agreed so the damned imperialists (the American ones
now) would leave.

TL;DR The United States lied going into the war in Cuba and
wouldn't get out until they got more than they were supposed
to get. People got pissed off accordingly. McKinley got elected
again anyway.

After peace was made with Spain, the U.S. looked towards better policies with the entire world. This started with John Hay, a U.S. diplomat, who noticed foreign interference with China and opened conversation just before the turn of the century to let the nation know that they had a friend in America. He was really making friends so we'd have more people to trade with, but the courtesy was still a nice touch.

In 1901, After McKinley was assassinated by some guy who hated government right after he was re-elected, Theodore Roosevelt became president and continued the government anyway. Teddy expanded U.S. foreign policy through his mantra of "speak softly and carry a big stick." This meant that first he would ask nicely and if that didn't work he'd fuck up countries with his stick. America's policy of listen-to-us-or-we'll-fuck-you-up-with-a-stick would stick around for a while. Teddy used this constant looming threat to get the U.S. more involved with global politics. He backed Panama revolutionaries in a revolt against Colombia in 1903, and the land that was taken over was given partially to Teddy to use for the Panama Canal. This was made possible by the Hay-Pauncefote Treaty of 1901, through which Britain canceled an older treaty that said Britain and the U.S. should share the canal zone. They didn't want to get fucked up by the big stick. Work started in 1904 and ten years later it was complete, giving the United States control over sea travel through Central America.

On the legal side, Roosevelt decided to whip out his stick and wave it at the Monroe Doctrine. He added the Roosevelt Corollary in 1904, which declared that whenever Europeans would try to mess with shit in Latin America, instead of just leaving it to Latin America to force them out, the United States would step up and fix shit for them. Over the next twenty years, however, Roosevelt pretty much just used his document to get countries to pay their debts on time. By the 1930s pretty much all of Latin America was pissed at the U.S.

Following his staunch policy of messing with shit in Latin America, Teddy next started messing with shit—though more subtly—in East Asia. After the Russo-Japanese war ended in 1905, Roosevelt arranged a meeting between the two bitter leaders on American ground, bringing us attention and credibility. In 1907, Roosevelt toured his "Great White Fleet" of freshly painted battleships around the world just to show off our new status. The U.S. got more involved in efforts to fuck things up and help other countries unfuck things they'd recently fucked up. It was all about being involved, and in 1908 results were finally tangible in the Root-Takahira Agreement, where the U.S. and Japan agreed officially to respect each other's territories and maintain an open door policy in China.

TL;DR Shit happened in East Asia and Latin America. John Hay started making moves to be friends with China, and Teddy Roosevelt used his "Big Stick" policy to solidify our free trade with China. Teddy also used it to make sure everybody in Latin America paid their debts, pissing everybody off but still getting a win by creating the Panama Canal and pushing America into the global spotlight.

TAFT'S FOREIGN POLICY

In the election of 1908, William Howard Taft, weighing in at a whopping 350 pounds, was elected after running against William Jennings Bryan (Populist guy with a silver fetish who was good at speeches). Considering how big Taft was, his stick certainly was...unproportional, and his foreign policy agenda known as "dollar diplomacy" was more about getting people to willingly invest in an expanding America (by backing internationally trading firms) than forcing people to pay off debt or get out of our way.

Taft tried his idea in 1911, by getting America a piece of an internationally-backed railroad building project in China, but got cucked by Japan and Russia soon after when they excluded the United States from another railroad project in the North. Taft's foreign policy was starting to look more like a shitty game of Monopoly. In 1912, Taft coldly watched the "Lodge Corollary" to the Monroe Doctrine pass, which basically decided that any country not in Europe didn't get to have land in the Western Hemisphere. This pissed some people off, including Russia and Japan, who were already ankle deep in American tears after the railroad incident.

TL;DR Taft, Roosevelt's successor, had a softer and more economics based foreign policy than Teddy, but it was still expansionist.

TAFT, TEDDY, PROGRESSIVISM AND EVERYONE ELSE INVOLVED IN IT

At home, Taft continued the domestic progressivism of his predecessor, a political concept characterized by the leaders' an unwavering urge for change, through his support for the 1910 Mann-Elkins act, which expanded the powers of the Interstate Commerce Commission, and the Sixteenth Amendment, known today for pissing off libertarians, which established a federal income tax. Roosevelt was a Type-A reformer, and so were the people around him. While Teddy was...

- Milking the Forest Reserve Act of 1891 to pump out national parks like nobody's business.

- Actually using the Sherman Antitrust Act of 1890 for "trust-busting"— i.e. breaking down big business conglomerates colluding to fuck over the consumer.

- Passing bills such as the Newlands Reclamation Act of 1902, which allowed for the sale of government owned land to western farmers, the Elkins act of 1903, that gave the Interstate Commerce Commission more authority to deal with shady railroad owners, and the Hepburn Act of 1906, which allowed the ICC to determine fair rail prices.

- Organizing a "square deal" between strikers and employers in the anthracite coal miner strike of 1902, in which he forced the mine-owners to actually listen to their employees and became very popular with labor because of it. The rest of the United States, having freshly regained its stomach for political life and activism, engaged in its own projects, including...

- Upton Sinclair, a "muckraker" journalist (which really just means a real life "meddling kid"), publishing *The Jungle,* a controversial tell-all book that depicted the grimey things he found while working in the Chicago meat-industry.

- Congress passing the *Pure Food and Drug Act* and *Meat Inspection Act* of 1906 (because people were pissed off by what they read in *The Jungle*).

- Other muckrakers getting involved and finally holding the industrial giants accountable, such as Chicago journalist Henry Demarest Lloyd, who wrote a series of articles and books (including his champion novel *Wealth Against Commonwealth* in 1894) on the corruption of the Standard Oil Company, and widely available publications such as *McClure's Magazine* competing to see who could best expose corruption in a consumer friendly way.

- Jane Addams working to develop one of the first settlement houses, an inner-city organization that worked to help the less fortunate in the area but also to lobby the government for reform in education, law, and at the time increasing parole, limiting usage of the death penalty, and more legally available divorce.

- Cities reforming themselves by instituting more voting for local positions as well as local governments buying public utility systems.

- Non-progressives campaigning for temperance on the state level, i.e. convincing state governments to ban the sale and consumption of alcohol.

- Citizens advocating for and transitioning to the secret ballot.

- William James' and John Dewey's advocacy for their "pragmatism" philosophy, that said truth could never be found in artsy/hippie shit and had to come from scientific trial and error, which called for a more involved and less "leave-us-the-fuck-alone" government policy.

- Frederick W. Taylor inputting his ideas by perfecting a system of "scientific management," that carefully choreographed how factory workers did each step of a job to cut out extra seconds of production time.

As I'm sure all that shit was hard for you to read, it was also hard for Taft to replicate, and many progressive Republicans thought he wasn't doing enough. Political enemies of Taft in his own party often cited his conservative-leaning biases, and gave Taft shit for failing to lower the Payne-Aldrich Tariff, which conservative Republicans supported and liberal Republicans heatedly opposed. In 1912, when Taft was nominated again by the Republicans, so many were pissed that Teddy Roosevelt was pressured to run as a progressive in the Bull Moose party, splitting the vote and giving Democrats for Wilson an easy win.

Woodrow Wilson, a Democrat who had a major god-complex, and the first one elected since Cleveland, considered himself invariably the man in charge. He wasn't about to take shit from anybody. Literally the first day he was president he lowered the tariff everyone was bitching about. In 1914, He ditched the gold standard in favor of the Federal Reserve Board, a sorta-government banking conglomerate that was meant to keep-up the stability the gold standard had failed to deliver, and created the Federal Trade Commission and Clayton Antitrust Act to back up what other legislation was struggling to do. Wilson would spend the latter half of his presidency, however, attempting to keep us out of WWI and failing (there's very little about any actual wars on standardized tests so don't worry too much about it, basically Germany sunk some American ships, *the Lusitania* and *The Sussex*, and then got caught red-handed in the Zimmermann Telegram incident, so we got pissed and took the side Germany wasn't on. Wilson also had "fourteen points" which he claimed would help keep peace in the future, centered on the claim that keeping communications between all nations healthy was vital). The era would close as Wilson passed the Selective Service Act, which began a draft lottery, and the Espionage and Sedition Acts, which questioned free speech and gave a paranoid government way more power over anyone talking shit—up to 20 years in prison.

Even while Wilson was occupied with the dawn of the war, however, other Americans were still focused entirely on the promises of the Progressive Era. It's list time once again...

- African-Americans were denied the era's prizes that Whites enjoyed due to growing prejudices, which were seemingly allowed and and supported by the government. Even so, leaders like W.E.B. Du Bois and Booker T. Washington took competing strides to garner Black self-support, with their respective ideals of immediate recognition for Black rights and gradual proof-of-place through education and economic prosperity.

- People migrated in droves to cities, where job opportunities were more open and more was going on at any given point than in the countryside.

- Civil Rights groups like the National Association for the Advancement of Colored People (NAACP) and National American Woman Suffrage Movement sprung up.

- Women fought for and won the right to vote (suffrage) with the Nineteenth Amendment in 1920 (would've been cooler if the 19th was passed in 1919, but I guess you can't have your cake and eat it too).

- Laws on divorce were eased after diligent lobbying. This helped a lot of women abandoned or abused by their husbands move on.

TL;DR The Progressive Era was all about people doing as much as possible. Politicians changed everything, and the people around them kept lobbying to prove there was more everything left to change. This went on from the beginning of the 20th century until WWI.

(1920-1929) THE ROARING TWENTIES: EVERYTHING IS GREAT BUT ALCOHOL IS ILLEGAL

A CORRUPT GUY WHO DOESN'T SAY ANYTHING IS PRESIDENT: THEN DIES

The twenties opened up with an election. Teddy Roosevelt had just died, WWI had just ended with the Treaty of Versailles (a big end-o'-war meeting where all the winners got to talk and all the losers had to listen) and the "progressive" energy of the Republican party was fading to economically moderate conservatives. In the running were Warren G. Harding, a quiet Republican who just said he wanted a "return to normalcy," and Gov. James Cox, a Democrat that wanted America to join the League of Nations and gave a fuck about actually campaigning and talking to people.

It was right after a war, so having goals, aspirations, and personality didn't really mean shit to the American people. Harding was elected. Harding surprised people by pardoning Eugene Debs, a socialist he had just run against in 1920 that was jailed for espionage (you might remember him from the Pullman strike a few chapters back), and by generally not being a god-awful president. He appointed some good people to his cabinet (along with a few incompetent ones that would end up causing a shitstorm of scandals) and basically just signed onto the laws that Congress' Republicans were creating, including an income tax reduction and a tariff increase bill. Luckily for Harding, he suddenly died in 1923, before anyone could blame him for causing the scandals that were really caused the people in his cabinet...that he chose.

TL;DR Warren Harding was elected. He didn't do much but be a boring Republican. Then he died.

A QUIETER GUY WHO'S NOT AS CORRUPT GETS THAT DEAD GUY'S JOB

Calvin "Silent Cal" Coolidge was Warren Harding's Vice President. So for a year after he died, Coolidge had to step up and become the big cheese of America. He employed a simple policy of telling government to get the fuck out of business affairs. Coolidge was nominated again in 1924, and defined his full presidency by actively not doing shit. Whenever a new law was introduced, Coolidge vetoed it if it got government more involved in the business world— even if it was introduced by the moderate Republican majority. He even vetoed bonuses proposed for WWI vets and the McNary-Haugen Bill of 1928, which was meant to help farmers get by as corn prices fell from the boom they had when extra crops were needed for the war. Coolidge did what he came to do: nothing. He was satisfied with this work and decided not to run again.

TL;DR Coolidge was Harding's VP. When Harding died, he got a promotion, ran again in 1924, and spent his one full term stopping the government from getting involved with the business world.

THE THIRD REPUBLICAN WITH THE DAM NAMED AFTER HIM

Herbert Hoover was up to bat, winning the Republican nomination in 1928. He'd been appointed to shit but never actually campaigned for anything. His opponent was supposed to be popular because he was against prohibition, but he was also a Catholic which people hated at the time. Republicans made a promise to continue Coolidge's years of prosperity, and Hoover even said he would end poverty entirely. Hoover of course won, like any good politician, by making empty promises that wouldn't mean a damn thing by the time he got in office. The unstoppable Great Depression rolled through just a year into Hoover's helpless administration, and these promises ended up not just broken, but ravaged.

TL;DR Hoover ran instead of Coolidge in 1928, talked big game, then got screwed by the big sad.

WHILE THESE GUYS WERE DOING NOTHING, EVERYTHING ELSE WAS HAPPENING

After a nice little post-war recession in 1921, the American economy exploded thanks to a number of factors. Research by Frederick W. Taylor on the science behind management was employed, as businessmen like Henry Ford began to utilize innovative mass production strategies like the assembly line. The oil and electricity markets grew as people relied more and more on the new technologies to run their homes. Low interest rates and the invention of credit caused people to just buy up all the shit they could get, because they knew they could always just pay for it later.

As wages rose, there was less of a need for unions, which had to fight harder anyway to change the very pro-business laws.

Pop culture became popular (hence the name). People were listening to experimental and rebellious Jazz music, watching sports and rooting for celebrity athletes, tuning into newfangled radio stations, and watching Hollywood movies.

Ironically, as the economy boomed, women's rights grew in every way except the labor force. Women were still expected to work in the home, but in their free time women and men alike experienced new sexual freedom, growing to fear premarital sex a little less and enjoy fucking a little more. 'Flappers' became a common nickname for girls who dressed in this promiscuous new manner, birth control became more acceptable than ever before, wives were finally allowed to initiate divorces, and women began to exercise the right to vote that had been won in 1920.

African-American culture exploded with the economy, as the Harlem Renaissance of— duh—Harlem, New York created a mosh-pit of Black art, literature, and music. Poets like Langston Hughes, Claude McKay, James Weldon Johnson, and Countee Cullen expressed the emotional experience of a disenfranchised minority in America. Jazz musicians like Duke Ellington and Louis Armstrong did the same thing but with weird music. Leaders like Marcus Garvey, who founded the United Negro Improvement Association, advocated to give Black Americans a voice, ranging from Garvey's calls for a 'return to Africa' to the echoes of historic leaders like W.E.B. Du Bois and Booker T. Washington, who pushed for immediate recognition of Black rights and gradualism through education respectively.

More controversial moves took place religiously. This guy named John T. Scopes tried to teach his students evolutionism in school. It was Tennessee, a very Christian state, so naturally he was arrested and brought to trial in 1925. Famous populist and Christian-as-fuck politician William Jennings Bryan was the prosecutor, and though he won the trial (kinda) he looked like such an idiot at some points (thanks to his silver tongued opponent: Clarence Darrow) that he literally died weeks later. Scopes wasn't actually punished for teaching evolution, but the trial proved that the constitution didn't really apply to people who weren't Christians.

Prohibition (A.K.A. the eighteenth amendment/the banning of alcohol), was also a real fucking bummer for the decade. The Volstead Act of 1919 provided for enforcement against the sale or possession of alcohol. Of course, nobody really gave too much of a fuck, and therefore breaking the rules became cool. This was especially easy to do, because the presidents at the time didn't give very much of a fuck either. Speakeasies became the new underground bars, and quick bribes to the fuzz kept them off party-goers backs. Prohibition wouldn't be canceled until FDR took office in 1933.

Racism and Xenophobia also permeated the twenties. As everyone really began to love their home America, Foreigners decided to immigrate and share that love. The locals saw this and decided to hate the immigrants for no real reason, leading to shitstorms of controversy, such as the execution of Nicola Sacco and Bartolomeo Vanzetti in 1927, who were convicted on iffy accusations of murder, which fell much short of being 'proven guilty.' The KKK reemerged in the boom, but so did efforts to stop it, leading to a giant hit in support when Grand Dragon David Stephenson (a stupid ass title, yes but he was really called that) was arrested for murder in 1925.

People were too happy with new luxuries, however, to really give a shit about domestic politics, and politicians weren't really concerned with them either, but there was still some foreign political shit going on that needed to be addressed.

In 1921, disarmament took center stage at the Washington conference, and three powerful treaties were established: the Five-Power Treaty, where five powerful navies agreed to disarmament, the Four-Power Treaty, where the U.S., France, Japan and Great Britain agreed to not fuck with each other's shit in the Pacific, and the Nine-Power Treaty, where everyone invited to that conference decided to keep the Open Door policy in China. The Kellogg-Briand Pact, probably the stupidest effort ever made, got a bunch of countries in 1928 to agree to just stop having wars. It didn't do shit, obviously. America got more involved in Latin America, Britain got more involved in the Middle-East, and people started tariffing

76

each other. Relations following WWI didn't heal overnight. In order to try and solve some of these problems, the Dawes plan of 1924 was put in place that handled the massive debt of Germany by lending Germany the money that they would use to pay everyone back. This just put Germany in more unsustainable debt, and the Ponzi Scheme-esq program went on until the stock market crashed and people realized that America couldn't just be giving away infinite money. This is part of why America became isolationist in the 30s.

TL;DR Crazy shit happened in the 20s. Black culture became more popular, so the KKK tried to also become more popular but got shut down. People bought shit they didn't need and put it on credit. Alcohol was banned but people didn't give a fuck. They were also racist and ignorant. Overall, there were mixed reviews on culture but the economy was booming so nobody really cared.

(1930-1945) THE DEPRESSION AND THE WAR: FUCK

THE GREAT DEPRESSION BEGINS

The Great Depression, triggered by a sudden stock market crash in 1929, was called the Great Depression because it was—duh—greater than other depressions. The U.S. economy had consistently had a cycle of ups and downs, but after the never-before-seen ups of the twenties, some big ass downs were geared up hot-n'-ready for the thirties.

Plenty of factors caused the Depression to be worse than any before. The farming industry had been declining since WWI, and now a drought added to the industry's struggles. Governments had been imposing tariffs on each other, holding back the trade needed to support their economies and foster good international relationships. Little regulation from Laissez-Faire capitalists had allowed for a lot of economic progress, but also a shit ton of malinvestment. The thing that brought the thirties crashing down was the wild credit bubble of the twenties. For the past ten years, a new system had been instituted where people only had to pay 10% of something's cost up front, and could pay the rest on credit over time. The problem was that this time would inevitably run out for the debtors, and people who couldn't afford to pay their debts would fall through, not only hurting the buyers of useless shit, but all the people who made wayyy too much useless shit in the first place. The global economy was also still in the toilet after WWI, which didn't help the situation. Hoover didn't really do shit in 1929 because he thought the crash would be over soon, and urged everybody else not to do shit either. That didn't help.

TL;DR All the prosperity of the twenties ended real fast in 1929 because most of the money spent in that decade couldn't be paid back. Hoover didn't know what was happening and acted accordingly.

DEPRESSION CONTINUES

Part of what made the Great Depression so great is that it was global. Hoover didn't help with this, and really fucked up bad when in 1930 he signed the Hawley-Smoot tariff, which put super high taxes on almost all foreign imports. The idea worked well to make sure domestic businesses didn't have foreign competition, except Hoover forgot that the rest of the world aren't idiots, and everyone else just tariffed us back harder. Due to this fuckery, we were so screwed that we had to cancel the Dawes plan in 1931, and Hoover passed a moratorium on debt, meaning that everybody would temporarily just not pay their debts. This fucked more shit up. Hoover tried to regain his footing when he realized in 1931 how bad he'd fucked up, but his efforts (expanding the power of the Federal Farm Board to help the agricultural industry and creating the Reconstruction Finance Corporation to help flailing infrastructure) weren't enough.

People got pissed. Farmers caused a fuss and in 1932, WWI vets who never got the bonuses they were promised marched on Washington D.C.. This ended up escalating when police killed two protesters, and Hoover ordered the area evacuated forcibly. People got more pissed, and the next year finally elected a Democrat.

TL;DR Everybody got hit hard by the Depression, Hoover made it worse and made himself look so bad we actually elected a Democrat.

THE GUY WITH THE SECRET POLIO

Franklin D. Roosevelt's campaign promised a "New Deal" for Americans. The message was good and all, but bottom line, it really didn't matter if he was good. It just mattered that he wasn't Herbert Hoover. Democrats, all of whom weren't Herbert Hoover, won both the presidency and control of Congress.

Their president himself, commonly abbreviated to FDR, was a weird guy. He grew up a preppy, posh only child and struggled to hide a debilitating disease as he ran for the Oval Office. His wife, Eleanor, was not just supporting Frank, but also making a name for herself as one of the most influential first ladies ever. Stuff was always going on for the Roosevelts.

FDR marketed his politics as a plan to reach "the three R's:" Relief (for the people), Recovery (for the economy), and Reform (for economic institutions). Roosevelt knew that he wouldn't be able to do all of this on his own, so he met regularly with a "Brain Trust," comprised of famous minds alongside anyone else he thought smart enough to give good advice. He was backed by so much knowledge (and dealing with such a loud call for change) that his first hundred days were more impactful than those of any president before him. He constructed a fuck-ton of new economic institutions: The Agricultural Adjustment Act (AAA), which sought to ease the farming industry from falling prices; The Civilian Conservation Corps (CCC), which provided jobs for single men, a large portion of the newly unemployed; The Federal Emergency Relief Administration (FERA) which provided states with help aiding

the unemployed; The Public Works Administration (PWA), which gave money to states for infrastructure jobs; the Tennessee Valley Authority (TVA), which was an experiment of federal investment into the energy industry of impoverished areas (particularly the Tennessee Valley); Jesus fuck take a break for the love of God there's way more; the Federal Deposit Insurance Corporation (FDIC) which backed individual bank deposits for up to $2500; the Home Owners Loan Corporation (HOLC) which helped refinance small homes; the Farm Credit Administration, which basically did the same shit with farms; the Emergency Banking Relief Act, which allowed the Fed's to investigate the finances of banks closed for the holiday; The National Recovery Administration (NRA) which allowed for price-fixing efforts to hold competition down; and FINALLY GODDAMN IT the Works Progress Administration (WPA), which employed Americans for public infrastructure construction and sometimes the arts. He was definitely doing more than Hoover.

In addition to all the aforementioned shit, FDR also called a bank holiday in 1933 to let things settle down, ended the gold standard to give monetary policy more flexibility, repealed prohibition that same year with the Twenty-First Amendment, and began his radio-broadcast "fireside chats" program.

FDR drove home the recovery aspect of his plan in his first two years in office. Moving forward, his focus shifted to the relief and reform sections of his promise. He bolstered his WPA program and gave loans to agricultural workers through a new organization called the Resettlement Administration. In a final sweep for progress, Roosevelt increased taxes on the wealthy, passed the National Labor Relations/Wagner Act of 1935, which finally offered legal protection for workers choosing to join a union and unions attempting to collectively bargain, and implemented required participation in government welfare with the Social Security Act of 1935. He ran again and was re-elected in 1936.

TL;DR FDR did fucking EVERYTHING that can possibly be done in his first term in office, but all of his actions were focused in the relief, recovery, and reform of the U.S.'s economy and labor force.

ROOSEVELT GETS ANOTHER TURN

Plenty of people disagreed with all the stuff Roosevelt was doing, notably Dr. Francis Townsend, who made suggestions on Social Security that FDR listened to and blended into his own ideas, Father Charles Coughlin, who hosted an Alex Jones-esq anti-FDR radio show, and extremists like Huey Long, who argued that FDR was taking a step in the right direction...towards communism.

The Supreme Court also gave FDR problems when he tried to stuff it full of Democrats with a new bill. People were pissed because all the other branches of government were already stuffed with Democrats. Roosevelt was forced to slow down.

Unions were growing thanks to FDR's earlier policies, but infighting became a problem, such as when the John L. Lewis headed Congress of Industrial Organizations branched off from the American Federation of Labor and the two became rivals. FDR's system became self

sustaining anyway, as workers employed strikes to get what they wanted instead of waiting for government-led changes. A maximum work week, child labor laws, and even a minimum wage were established. Things were moving forward, and now with joint leadership between Republicans and Democrats.

Foreign Policy wise, Roosevelt was all about a Good Neighbor Policy, which was great because America had been using a Shit Neighbor Policy since the turn of the century. In 1933, he worked in the Pan-American conferences to assure Latin America that the U.S. would stop fucking with its internal affairs. He canceled the Platt Amendment too, which got America way too involved with Cuba. Also in 1933, Roosevelt supported the London Economic Conference, until it started saying shit about not manipulating currencies for national gain and he bailed because that was his entire plan. FDR helped grow Filipino independence, recognized the USSR, and worked to build trade agreements. These were especially important overtures to make, because as will be explained later, everybody else's shitty attitude made FDR's efforts look especially noble.

TL;DR In term two, FDR made sure we were nice to the rest of the world and lost his footing a little, but recovered by continuing his policy of actually doing shit.

JUST HOW DEPRESSING WAS IT

The depression truly was depressing. Unemployment was as high as 25% in some places, and this left little gap for the Women/African-Americans presence needed to take down workplace discrimination. Roosevelt personally employed many African-American men, but nobody in the private sector was working to solve the problem until Union leader A. Philip Randolph threatened a march on Washington. In 1941, the Fair Employment Practices Committee was established to help ease this tension. Agriculture suffered despite FDR's efforts, as the "Dust Bowl" drought hit the great plains in the early thirties and further fucked up many crops that were already struggling to survive.

The economy was in the shitter, and everything was going so wrong that immigrants, such as Mexican-Americans, just packed up and went home to look for work. One of the only wins came when John Collier, the new commissioner of the Bureau of Indian affairs, got the Indian Reorganization (AKA

Wheeler-Howard) Act passed in 1934, that gave Native-Americans back some land and canceled the Dawes-Severalty Act of 1887.

TL;DR The Depression hit harder as minorities were disenfranchised, a quarter of everyone was unemployed, and farmers got hit with the "Dust Bowl," which is about as bad for farming as it sounds.

MEANWHILE, SHIT'S GOING ON IN EUROPE: AMERICA TRIES TO STEER CLEAR

While the Great Depression did spread to the rest of the world, America was the only country that really had time to give a shit because everybody else was too busy being problematic.

Problems started in 1931, when Japan invaded the Manchuria in China, and the U.S. enacted the Stimson Doctrine, in which it officially decided that this invasion didn't mean anything. This pissed people off, and Japan would remember it for later.

In Germany, Adolf Hitler, resident bitch, stopped paying reparations and doing pretty much everything the Treaty of Versailles told him to do. He made friends with Benito Mussolini, the fascist dictator of Italy, and together they started a general takeover of Europe. Europe, however, decided to appease the bitch, in an effort—well, a lack of effort—known as (duh) appeasement. The more powerful countries in Europe just nervously watched as Hitler and Mussolini committed crimes that were egregiously bad, but not quite big enough for anybody to intervene.

In 1935, Mussolini invaded Ethiopia. The League of Nations said this was wrong, but let him do it anyway. In 1936, Hitler took the Rhineland, a place between France and Germany that the Treaty of Versailles claimed should permanently demilitarized, and militarized it. In 1938, Germany planned to invade the Sudetenland, a very German part of Czechoslovakia. Roosevelt didn't like this, so he encouraged a meeting between Neville Chamberlain (Prime Minister of

Britain), Édouard Daladier (President of France), Hitler, and Mussolini. (Czechoslovakia wasn't invited and was pissed off accordingly). The men met in Munich in 1938, and agreed to let Hitler have the Sudetenland as long as the Germans promised to stop fucking shit up in the rest of Europe. Germany proceeded to take the Sudetenland, an area central to Czechoslovakian defense efforts, and then proceeded almost immediately to fuck shit up for the rest of Europe, including Czechoslovakia. What a bitch.

Japan was doing its own shit in Asia, and went to war with China in 1937. During the invasion, Japan accidentally sunk an American ship, for which it apologized. They would become a problem later on, but for now the United States and Japan had little interest in fighting each other because too much other shit was going on.

TL;DR Back in Europe, Hitler started taking shit over with Mussolini. Everybody else thought this was wrong but nobody cared enough to do anything about it, especially America. This is called "appeasement." Japan started their own conquests but nobody cared about that enough to do anything either.

WORLD WAR TWO IS STARTING: FUCK?

At the dawn of World War Two, the United States was semi-grateful. On one hand,

thousands of innocent people were dying. On the other hand, they were other people from

other countries, and we are/were capitalists. Now that the war was underway, there was work to be done. President Roosevelt greatly increased the budget for national defense in the second half of the 1930s (a trend America continues with today) and factories were reopened as weapons became the States' new cash crop. The urgency for war supplies gave even women had a chance to get involved. Propaganda became an economy with in itself, running wild to support all of war industry, and the soon to be unleashed "Office of War Information" did...exactly what it sounds like it does. We would be manufacturing information as fast as we manufactured weapons.

Unfortunately, at the start of the war, America couldn't do shit with all those extra weapons we made because we had already signed up for the Neutrality Acts, preventing us from selling weapons to any foreign countries who were fighting the war...A.K.A the people that would want to buy those weapons the most. Roosevelt, like any good president, did his best to trick Congress, and in 1939 he convinced them that selling weapons to other countries didn't count as breaking neutrality if those countries came here to get the weapons, paid upfront, and brought them back on their own. This was unsurprisingly called "Cash and Carry."

Though the "Cash and Carry" policy was technically fair game to any country willing to make the trip, it helped Britain the most because only British (and British-allied) ships could make the trip without being attacked by all the other British Ships. The British Navy was still powerful, and during World War Two it really got its ships together (pun intended). By 1941, the "Cash" part of "Cash and Carry" was dropped, and weapons were sold on credit in the new "Lend-Lease" system.

TL;DR Manufacturing weapons for WWII began to rebuild the American economy. When America needed places to sell the weapons, it started to slowly break the neutrality it had based its foreign policy on for the past twenty years, erring towards the British.

AMERICA PICKS A SIDE

More changes came as Roosevelt was elected for his third term in 1940. The Selective Service Act of 1940 legalized the peacetime draft, preparing the population for war the same way industry had been prepared: government force. That same month, FDR organized a deal with Britain, trading them fifty Destroyer ships for privileges to build bases on British-owned islands. Nobody had officially admitted that the U.S. was now supporting Britain...but the U.S. was sure as shit supporting

Britain.

Roosevelt began to rebrand America's foreign policy as the world's "Arsenal of Democracy." In January of 1941, he delivered a speech about freedom that was really a speech about lending the British government money so they could afford to buy the American weapons...by giving that money back to America. It was basically just a complicated way of giving them free weapons. FDR met in secret with Winston Churchill, the Prime Minister of Britain at the time, to discuss a long-term plan for peace called the "Atlantic Charter." FDR

followed this meeting up by ordering U.S. Navy ships to act as escorts for British "Lend- Lease" ships. German submarines decided to shoot at one of these ships (*The Greer*), which turned out to be a major fuck-up as Roosevelt just decided (kinda illegally) that now we could shoot any and all German subs on sight. Germany continued to fuck with America's escort ships, so the Lend-Lease policy—designed to keep America out of the conflict—no longer meant shit and was abandoned accordingly.

While connections to the British side were growing, relationships with the Axis powers were falling apart. Japan joined the Axis in 1940, which caused FDR to ban selling steel and iron to all countries except Britain, basically subtweeting Japan. Japan, intending to use these metals to take over the world and kill innocent people, got mad and said that America was being "unfriendly." To prove that it could wave its dick around even without American steel, Japan invaded French-controlled Indochina. Roosevelt became less subtle and halted all oil sales to Japan. This was further fucking things up, however, because without American oil, Japan was only more rushed to invade the countries that they could steal oil from.

General Hideki Tojo tried to negotiate throughout October of 1941. When that didn't work, Japan instead launched a surprise attack on Pearl Harbor on December 7th, killing 2400 people and destroying 170 military vehicles. Yikes.

TL;DR Roosevelt decided that in his third term the United States would continue to passive aggressively side with Britain, mainly through economic policy, and become increasingly obvious about it. Tensions grew with Japan because of this, which resulted in the Japanese surprise attack on Pearl Harbor.

AMERICA JOINS THE WAR

Roosevelt was pissed off from Pearl Harbor, as were most Americans, and immediately wanted to declare war, so we officially joined the Atlantic Charter, and roped Germany and Italy into our conflict. About time we actually did something.

We won. Yay! (Don't worry your pretty little head off about military history, just read these bullet points about it).

Stuff during/after the war that actually matters:

- Tehran Conference (1943): FDR, Joseph Stalin, (in charge of Russia, kind of a major   commie but we put our differences aside for a few years) and Winston Churchill, PM of Great Britain, meet. They discussed important shit such as the opening of a second front and the USSR helping against Japan once Germany lost. The second front issue led to the invasion of France in '44.

- Dumbarton Oaks Conference: It already has dumb in its name. Pretty much all that happened was that America, Britain, the USSR, and China drew up the General Assembly/Security Council that we have today, but it was a lot of wasted time for not much progress in the war.

- The Yalta Conference (Feb. 1945): Same people as Teheran. They talked about a lot more stuff this time:

- Poland was an issue. The USSR had put its own government there, but we still weren't exactly keen on the Commies expanding their sphere of influence. We decided that Russia would get more territory, but agreed that they should only enstate a coalition government. Wonder how well that worked out.

- Germany next. We decided that after the Allies won (which we would), Germany would be split it into four zones and watched over in a joint effort between the winners. We also decided on lots of preliminary reparations (most of which went to the USSR for all the men they lost).

- The Smith Connally Anti-Strike Act of 1943 granted the government permission to take over war-related businesses whose industry was threatened by a strike. It was passed over Roosevelt's veto. So much for unions.

- D-Day! The exclamation here isn't the good kind of excitement, it's just there to note how important June 6th, 1944, A.K.A D-Day, is. The D-Day Invasion was one of the bloodiest and most important days of WWII, in which Allied forces took the offensive and invaded France through the beaches of Normandy. It was a turning point for sure, but the price was 425,000 lives.

In other news, we couldn't exactly pay for the obscene cost of the war, so the U.S. government literally just sold debt ("give us a hundred bucks to kill some Nazis today, we'll give you a thousand bucks when somebody else gets elected and has to pay it") through war bonds...not our best long term idea, but the bonds helped out for a while when we really needed cash. The war, which was primarily about killing minority groups, actually helped American minorities. African-Americans were given more opportunities and incentivized to migrate north from southern states. The NAACP grew exponentially, and the *Smith vs Allwright* case determined that denying African-Americans membership to political parties (to prevent them from voting in primaries) wasn't *Allwright* at all (haha but seriously). The Mexican-American demographic grew as immigration boomed from the war-based job opportunities, but this trend ended up starting the Zoot Suit riots of 1943, as angry White assholes wanted to fight Mexican-Americans for...being in America (particularly in L.A.). Japanese-Americans, however, were sadly but majorly fucked, because after Japan attacked Pearl Harbor, many loyal Japanese-Americans were nonetheless treated like the enemy, often thrown into internment camps along the west coast. The Supreme Court upheld the practice in the 1944 case *Korematsu v. The U.S.*.

General Dwight D. Eisenhower, meanwhile, was gaining fame by working with British General Bernard Montgomery to retake North Africa in Operation Torch, which lasted from 1942-43. While Eisenhower was setting his sights on Italy down south, American planes were bombing the shit outta Germany in the north.

We beat back Germany, giving the Soviets the final blow to keep them happy for now...we knew they'd be our next enemy. The rest of the war was just fighting island-hopping battles in Japan in the Pacific Theatre, until we finally finished them off with two atom bombs to Hiroshima and Nagasaki in the summer of 1945.

TL;DR The Second World War went pretty well. America joined in late but ended up on the winning side, Roosevelt took his time and planned really well, and we even ended up getting along pretty well with Commies for the sake of the cause.

The people elected Roosevelt again in 1944, partially because they were in the middle of the war that he had tons of experience with, and partially because his Republican competition was boring-ass Thomas Dewey. He only lived three months into his term (remember the secret Polio thing), and most of the war clean up efforts would be handled by his Vice- President, Harry Truman.

Under Truman, things just kinda wrapped up. Eisenhower led the bloody but successful D-Day invasion of Normandy in June, and by the end of the summer Paris was freed. Germany's last offensive attack, The Battle of the Bulge, didn't really do shit to help them, but it was still important because it was their last one. It took place in December of 1944. Hitler, ever a bitch, finally killed himself in April of 1945 to avoid being killed by other people. Eisenhower let our Soviet allies finish off the Germans because we were gonna need them not to do their communist shit later on, so this was a way to gain some credit by passing them the torch. Official German surrender came on May 7th, so for some reason May 8th is now

"Victory in Europe Day."   Europeans weren't the only people fighting, however. On the Japanese front, the war

was winding down as the United States fucked up their whole navy in the Battle of Leyte Gulf (October 1944). The Japanese counter-fucked us up by using Kamikaze pilots to mess with our planes, but in doing this they also fucked themselves up further. Both sides suffered major losses as the U.S. delivered their final land based attack, in the Battle of Okinawa (April to June of 1945).

Harry Truman saw how bloody things were getting and thought that disintegrating the blood would be a better way to fight. He told Japan that they should surrender or face "utter destruction." Japan didn't surrender, so he utterly destroyed them, dropping our new super expensive Atom Bombs, brought to you by Robert Oppenheimer (sounds like the kinda guy who would develop the Atomic Bomb) on two Japanese cities: Hiroshima, and Nagasaki days later. The bombs were dropped in August, but Japan didn't surrender until a month later, on the condition that we allowed the Emperor of Japan to keep his title (but none of the power). That was a weird one.

Decisions made in the various conferences were put into play. As discussed in Yalta, Germany would be divided into occupation zones, and the organization that would become the United Nations was born. The Potsdam conference, which was held in late July after Germany's surrender and is where Truman got the idea to threaten Japan, enacted its second plan of holding trials for Nazi war-criminals. Potsdam is important not only because it set the plan for ending the war into motion, but because it was the first time Truman no longer had to sit at the kiddie table and could actually attend an international meeting.

As the war ended, people got kinda pissy over time because they realized that it had not only caused over a million American casualties, but had caused U.S. debt to grow to quintuple its original size. By October of 1945, America agreed to rules set by the new United Nations and became involved, showing just how much more impact this war had than the Great War (WWI) itself.

TL;DR FDR got elected, then he died in 1945. Truman took over, beat Germany in D-Day and the Battle of the Bulge, and then beat Japan with two of Oppenheimer's special Atom Bombs. After the war we realized that a LOT of people died. We made more of an effort to not do that anymore by joining the U.N..

(1945-1960) THE COLD WAR STARTS RIGHT AFTER WWII
ENDS: 'CAUSE FUCK PEACE

THE DEAD GUY'S REPLACEMENT STARTS GETTING SHIT
DONE... OR AT LEAST SHIT WAS GETTING DONE
AROUND HIM

As the second World War ended, everyone was in a recovery
phase from the shitstorm we'd all just gone through.

America was doing pretty well—duh, we fucking won—and
even as soldiers lost their jobs in the field, the economic
recovery from the Great Depression allowed for them to find
jobs that were being created all over the place. America had
rebuilt its work ethic, and as things calmed down Americans
wanted to buy the luxuries they were producing. People moved
into suburbs, the government built the highways to get there,
and everyone bought a car. Life was good going into and
throughout the fifties, especially compared to how shitty it was
in the forties...and thirties.

In 1944, the GI bill, A.K.A. the Servicemen's Readjustment
Act, was passed and helped out by giving stipends for
education to returning soldiers as they eased their way back
into the working world. The bill also helped the soldiers get
loans to buy homes and start businesses. With prosperity
comes fucking, and with the forties and fifties comes virtually
no birth control, so tons of babies were born in the decade
following the war. That's why they're called "Baby Boomers."
It's America, so women were very pressured to take care of
these babies, but even so, women in the workforce grew a lot.

Weird shit started happening as highways rolled in and
transport was taking over, and people in America—for the first
time but not really the first time—started moving en masse to
other places in America, particularly sunny places with low
taxes. Everybody wanted to see some palm trees.

Truman passed the Employment Act in 1946, which created a
Council of Economic Advisors to support his goals of raising

the minimum wage and getting everybody a job (which really doesn't ever work unless you print a bunch of money, which causes a fuck ton of other problems). He also passed the National Security Act of 1947, which helped grow and reorganize our military. On the European side, he pushed forward the Marshall Plan that same year, which basically just sent money to Europe to help it rebuild itself.

Truman had to deal with the fact that money was already being devalued, however, and tried to make a continuation of price controls to keep inflation low. It didn't work, because most Congressmen didn't agree with him, and inflation ended up at rates as high as 25% (that's really fucking high). Truman didn't want to deal with anybody's shit after he got wrecked by Congress and turned out to be right anyway. In turn, he was very tough on strikes and went hard on civil rights reform, helping to desegregate government, schools, and the military all at once.

The Republicans were in control of Congress with democratic Truman in the White House, so conflicts like these were bound to happen. In 1947, the Congress passed the Taft- Hartley Act over Truman's veto, which basically really fucked up shit for unions. Truman was pissed off and called it a "slave-labor bill."

Truman won a second term in 1948, and since nobody forgot about FDR's ball-hogging the White House, the Republicans passed the twenty-second Amendment in 1951, imposing a two-term limit on all future presidents.

The president picked up the pace in term two and began work on his "Fair Deal" plan, which was trying to build off of FDR's "New Deal," now that it wasn't really new anymore. He pushed for national health insurance, education spending, more civil rights stuff, public housing programs, etc. He basically just wanted the government to spend more money on shit. A lot of these ideas didn't work because he had to go through Congress, and he didn't have energetic support from the people, because everybody was distracted by the foreign chill of the impending Cold War...

TL;DR After the war ended, America was prosperous, Europe was…getting there, and Truman struggled to do as much as possible with the economic boom that was happening. People also made a lotta goddamn babies.

THE COLD WAR BEGINS ABROAD

A lot of people are confused about the Cold War because it wasn't actually cold, it wasn't actually a war because nobody fought, and it's pretty unclear when it started and ended. Confusing, right. Either way, it's widely accepted that America's Cold War began after WWII, so now's a pretty good time to talk about it in the book.

Russia was no longer our ally after the war ended, so it naturally became our enemy because…communism. Some shit went down in the U.N. and things started to get tense right after WWII. In 1946, the Soviets didn't exactly *invade* the countries around them, but the ones they were already occupying…they kinda just didn't leave. The Soviets basically put a bunch of communist dictators in charge of Eastern Europe, which pissed off the Brits and Americans. The USSR also refused to abandon their "temporary" occupation of Germany, which resulted in the literal Berlin Wall being erected (hehehe) along with the metaphorical "Iron Curtain," that Churchill used to describe the divide between communist Europe and capitalist Europe. Truman pushed a policy of containment, which means exactly what it sounds like. He wanted to contain communism, not letting it spread any further into Europe or anywhere else in the world. He worked with his secretary of state, General George Marshall, to make figure out how to make that happen. Along with the Marshall plan to rebuild Europe, Truman's squad made other efforts, such as the 1948 Berlin Airlift, where America realized that Soviet walls couldn't stop them from just dropping shit by airplane over the city. Stalin wasn't willing to fight back and gave into peer pressure, slightly opening up the borders by 1949.

The Truman doctrine was another move by—duh—Truman,

which gave money to "free people" (non communists) in Turkey and Greece to fight "totalitarians" (commies). Additionally, Truman made the decision to enter the U.S. into NATO (North Atlantic Treaty Organization) and used the new group to position North American troops in Western Europe. The Soviets countered with the Warsaw pact, which basically did the same thing but in the East. Truman counter-countered with the National Security Act of 1947, that furthered American efforts in the arena by reorganizing the military at home, including the addition of two new military programs: The National Security Council and the Central Intelligence Agency.

As tensions grew between the capitalists and communists, so did the number of weapons each side had. By 1949 the Soviets had tested their own uber-powerful bomb, the Hydrogen-Bomb, which was a major step up from the Atomic-Bomb. Both sides spent more and more, acquiring newer and scarier weapons, though neither intended to actually use them because the other side could strike back with the same intensity.

Like WWII, the Cold War reached into the depths of the Asian continent too. Japan was basically under the United States' thumb with General Douglas MacArthur, a notorious hardass, running shit. In 1951 they signed the U.S.-Japanese Security Treaty, which basically just said the U.S. would not threaten Japan's security anymore if they gave up Korea, and led to the U.S. ending Japanese occupation later that year. Japan was the United States' bitc— valued ally. We set up American military bases in Japan and the Philippines, strengthening our support in the hemisphere.

Mao Zedong, a communist revolutionary in China, was in the midst of a civil war that had been put on pause when Japan was trying to take over China in the thirties and early forties. Truman obviously didn't want a commie to win, so he sent George Marshall to negotiate peace talks in 1946. It didn't work, and as the capitalists started to lose power, Truman gave them a bunch of money and supplies in 1948...that the communists would just steal from them anyway: the old switcheroo. America does this a lot. Truman was petty and decided just to not acknowledge Mao's China for a whole thirty years. Instead of looking for U.S. help, Mao signed the Sino-Soviet pact with Stalin in 1950, solidifying his communist bonds.

While all this went down, a little Korean war happened on the side. After Japan gave up Korea in exchange for peace, Korea was split into the Soviet controlled North and the U.S. controlled South, which wouldn't be peaceful at all. When North Korea surprise attacked the South in June of 1950, the U.N. sent troops to help the South that were pretty much just American soldiers. Just as the North seemed to clinch it, MacArthur counter-surprise attacked from behind by water, and pushed the North almost all the way back to China, who threatened to start fucking people up if the U.N didn't step back. Eventually fighting stabilized at the 38th parallel, splitting North and South back up just like they started. Truman was cool with this but MacArthur started throwing temper tantrums to the press and got fired for insubordination. As Eisenhower took office in 1943, the talks wound down into an Armistice, and the only thing left of the war was an excuse to say containment worked and drastically grow the military.

TL;DR The Cold War started with Truman putting troops in Western Europe, as Stalin put troops in—you guessed it—Eastern Europe. The U.S. took over Japan, made Japan give up Korea, stepped out of Japan, then had to step into Korea where things got messy. Korea got even more messy when the U.S. received a whooping from the communist Chinese, who's leader the U.S. had pissed off by pretending they didn't exist.

THE COLD WAR BACK AT HOME

A second "Red Scare" took root in the late 1940s, and this time, people got just scared enough to kind of do something about it. In 1947, the Loyalty Order was set up by Truman to do background checks (for communism) on 3 million government employees, causing tons of resignations and firings through the early fifties.

The Smith Act of 1940 (which the supreme court held up in *Dennis et al. v. United States*) subtly furthered this cause by making it illegal to encourage overthrowing the government, and just as illegal to be in an organization that was threatening to. This escalated further with the McCarran Internal Security Act of 1950, another Act passed over Truman's veto, that basically said if you talk shit about capitalist government or hire people who talk such shit, you are breaking the law and can be put in detention camps for said shit-talkers. The Un-American Activities Committee (mhm, so creative!) worked to weed out commies in everything from the Boy Scouts to the entertainment industry.

All this big talk began to mean something when it actually started fucking up people's lives. When Alger Hiss, a hot shot who worked with FDR, was sentenced for perjury in 1950, people started to get scared that anyone could be a commie, even the high ups in Washington D.C.. Julius and Ethel Rosenberg were executed in 1953 for being communist spies, even though there wasn't really any proof that Ethel was a communist spy. Cases like this pissed people off on both sides, capitalists were mad that the Loyalty Order was becoming an unreliable witch hunt, and communists were upset because...well...they were the ones being hunted.

The man at the top of the food chain for commie-hunters was Wisconsin Senator Joseph McCarthy. In 1950, McCarthy basically claimed that everybody in the State Department was a communist, and became really popular because people hated communists. In 1954 however, millions watched as his accusations finally were put to the test in the Army-McCarthy hearings...and as everyone finally realized he was a hardass bullshitter and began to hate McCarthy almost as much as the commies.

TL;DR People got scared about commies again, but thanks to the wonders of television, they only had to attack a few hundred innocent people before they realized that there wasn't anything to be afraid of.

EISENHOWER

After Truman decided not to run again, following one messy-ass hell of a presidency, Dwight "Ike" Eisenhower brought one in for the Republicans in 1952.

Ike got in office by promising to visit Korea and put an end to the war. People were tired of wars by the fifties. They didn't give a fuck about winning them, just ending them. The Koreas signed an armistice within a year. People liked Ike.

Domestically, Ike was a compromising and moderate conservative. He made major efforts to curb the deficit spending we had seen from the past 20 years of Democratic Party leaders (It didn't work perfectly, but at least he gave more than the half assed efforts everybody else would give). He also grew social security and the welfare system as a whole, organizing the new Department of Health, Education, and Welfare, of which he delegated authority to Oveta Culp Hobby, the first Republican cabinet woman. Eisenhower also pushed the Highway act of 1956, which created the infrastructure needed to backup the economy, that all of a sudden was growing fast as fuck.

The only "fighting" going on in the Cold War under Ike was pretty much between him and his Secretary of State, John Dulles. Dulles wanted a policy of "massive retaliation," where the U.S. mainly just makes a fuck ton of nukes incase we need to fight, whereas Eisenhower wanted nukes but didn't want to blow up the whole fucking universe. So they compromised and developed the hydrogen bomb in 1953.

While gigantic bombs are great for commies, it's not really worth it to use nukes in tiny battles in other countries. Instead, Ike used covert action from the CIA to meddle in third-world affairs. This pissed people off, duh, and in 1958 crowds in Venezuela tried to attack VP Richard Nixon out of bad-blood. This could've just been because Richard was a dick, though (pun intended, but it's true).

Meanwhile, other shit was happening in Vietnam. The country was temporarily split in half following the Geneva Conference, Ho Chi Minh (the guy, not the city) was the commie leader of the North and Ngo Dinh Diem the capitalist leader of the South. Eisenhower employed his new idea of the "domino theory," that if one country becomes communist all the countries around it will follow, and so on, to justify the United States giving South Vietnam over a billion dollars from 1955 on to help fight the commies. Dulles stepped in to help and formed the Southeast Asia Treaty Organization (SEATO), in which a bunch of Southeast Asian countries agreed to help each other fend off attacks from commies.

Double meanwhile, even more shit was happening in the Middle East. General Gamal Nasser in Egypt asked the U.S. for money to build a dam. America said no, so they turned petty and got the money from the Soviets instead. Nasser wanted even more fucking money though so he attacked and took Suez Canal, on Egyptian land, from the Brits and French in 1956. Britain, France, and our new ally Israel took the canal back pretty quickly, but the Suez Crisis was nonetheless important because Ike just wouldn't stop bitching about it, our allies Britain and France almost got us in trouble with the Soviets, and it was all for basically nothing because our European friends were forced to back down anyway. Now that he had his masculinity attacked, Ike kicked it up a notch with the Middle East, and created the Eisenhower Doctrine in 1957 that offered free money and help to any Middle Eastern country fighting off (or soon to be fighting off) commies.

Triple meanwhile, even more fucking shit was going down with the Soviets and Cuba. In 1953, Ike presented his "atoms for peace" plan to the U.N., where basically we'd try on both sides to make things less tense. Eisenhower met with Nikolai Bulganin, leader of the USSR, in Geneva in 1955 to follow up, and presented an "open skies" plan that would allow for aerial photography from other nations. The Soviets rejected the idea, because it was obviously just a blatant ploy to spy on them, but the peaceful, productive meeting made us a little cooler with them anyway. When the USSR launched the two Sputnik satellites into orbit in 1957, America overreacted by a whole fucking lot and, in 1958, not only was NASA created and billions spent towards its efforts, but the National Defense and Education Act was also signed, which gave hundreds of millions of dollars towards math and foreign language studies...hmm. Another crisis was brewing in Berlin, but instead of dealing with it Ike met in Camp David with Khrushchev, the next new USSR leader, and decided to put off the entire issue and just meet again on the subject in 1960. Just before that meeting, a U-2 spy plane that America had sent to take aerial pics of the USSR (not giving a shit that they specifically told us not to do that in 1955), was captured. Ike said sorry but it wasn't good enough...Kruschev wasn't mad, just disappointed, and had to cancel the Paris summit.

Closer to home, Fidel Castro had just taken power in Cuba in 1959. Castro communismed all over Cuba's face, so Eisenhower got mad and embargoed Cuba. Castro in turn just decided to make an ally with the Soviets, which would end up being very problematic for the next few presidents. Leaving office after 8 years, and having grown the military enough for it to take part in all the bullshit going on everywhere, Eisenhower warned in his farewell address that we should be careful about growing the military a lot and taking part in all the bullshit going on everywhere. The concept he feared was named the "military- industrial complex," a term that podcasters still use today.

TL;DR Ike stopped the Korean war, grew welfare, got the CIA mixed up in shit it wasn't supposed to be mixed up in, made a couple communist enemies, eased tensions with the biggest communists but then made some of that tension come back a year later, and warned America not to repeat his mistakes.

ALL THE OTHER SHIT THAT HAPPENED WHILE EISENHOWER WAS PRESIDENT

The momentum Truman built through his vigorous civil rights reform, combined with the economic impact of the post-war boom, brought a lot of cultural growth from 1952-1960 that Eisenhower didn't really have a major hand in. African-Americans, who went so far as migrating to northern cities as to avoid southern discrimination, were slowly and controversially gaining more liberties across the board. One really fucking goddamn important as FUCK thing for you to know for the life/standardized U.S. history tests is the supreme court case *Brown v. The Board of Education of Topeka*, in which Thurgood Marshall and a bunch of other NAACP lawyers ended the legality of segregation in 1954 (reversing the 1896 ruling in *Plessy v. Ferguson*). Southern White people decided that they should be total dickasses about this, and started fighting back against the new orders to desegregate schools. The biggest dickass by far was Arkansas Governor Orval Faubus, who in 1956 used the literal fucking Arkansas National Guard to stop *nine* Black students from going to class at Little Rock Central High School. Ike had to step in to shut him down, but the national government involved, southern states weren't afraid to literally close down a bunch of public schools just so Black kids couldn't attend. In 1955, when Rosa Parks was arrested for refusing to move to the back of a bus in Montgomery, Alabama, a boycott of the city's buses ensued until a 1956 supreme court ruling backed up the protestors. Seeing a pattern?

Inspired by events like these, nonviolent protests from the Black community were growing. Dr. Rev. Martin Luther King Jr. founded the Southern Christian Leadership Conference in 1957, which organized churches and ministries to stand together for civil rights. The Student Nonviolent Coordinating Committee was founded as well in 1960, and used sit-ins and other forms of protest to get shit done and get discrimination over with.

On the brighter side of things, the economy was growing fanatically. Television became a thing. Advertising became a big thing. People read paperback books and played records while they read, even religion got a piece of the action. Important people here are Will Herberg, who wrote a book called *Protestant, Catholic, Jew* in 1955 that observed the new religious flexibility and tolerance of the time, and William Whyte, who wrote about how corporate America was killing individuality in his 1956 book *The Organization Man.*

Sociologist C. Wright got ballsy and wrote not one but TWO books, *White Collar* in 1951 and 92

The Power Elite in 1956, both pretty much about how big businesses and crazy governments are bad. Finally, J.D. Salinger wrote the book everybody has to read now in high school, *The Catcher in the Rye,* in 1956.

The pinnacle of counterculture in the fifties was a niche group known as the Beatniks, who basically shared everything, from drugs to sex partners, and were rebels without any real cause. Notable beatniks were poet Allen Ginsberg and author Jack Kerouac. That's pretty much all you need to know about them. They shouldn't mind sharing the spotlight of this chapter, anyway.

TL;DR In the fifties, African-Americans and women looked for more rights, African-Americans had some success. Everybody bitched about it. The economy grew a lot too, which tons of people found a way to bitch about, especially now that books were more popular.

(1960-) PERSONALITY IN POLITICS: IF YOU DON'T HAVE IT, YOU'RE FUCKED

JOHN BEATS DICK, A DICK BEATS JOHN

In the 1960 election, Democrat John F. Kennedy took down Eisenhower's VP Richard (Dick) Nixon by a handful of votes. He won because he looked better on TV (not kidding, polls said that the majority of people who listened to their debate on the radio liked Nixon best, but those who saw the men on T.V. were way more into JFK).

Kennedy's goals were to grow funding for education and healthcare, as well as to support civil rights, and his lofty dreams combined with personal charm formed a "new frontier" for American politics. He didn't actually get much shit done domestically, but his VP Lyndon B. Johnson did after JFK was assassinated in 1963 (by a dick, probably Lee Harvey Oswald). JFK's focus in his few years as president was really all the international shit to get done. In 1961, he set up the Peace Corps to get American volunteers to help out developing nations, as well as the Alliance for Progress, which helped Latin American countries economically. Despite these wins, '61 was still a god-awful year for Kennedy, as he really fucked up the Bay of Pigs invasion. He sent CIA-trained Cuban exiles back to Cuba to attack the commies, they got stuck, and when Kennedy panicked and didn't send any back up they got slaughtered. The bungle gave Castro a stronger bond with the Soviets and obviously a weaker bond with us. After this tragedy Kennedy met with Soviet leader Khrushchev in Vienna, and they started fighting again about whether America should leave Berlin, a conversation Ike had cleverly avoided. We didn't leave the city, so the Soviets got mad and built a wall to keep us out of their half and their business.

In 1962, the good news was the Trade Expansion Act being passed, that lowered tariffs for America and Europe. The bad news was the Cuban Missile Crisis. It's pretty much what it sounds like. The United States found secret missile launching sites the Soviets built in Cuba. Kennedy pulled a power move and blockaded Cuba, which forced Kruschev—after a few really tense, fucked up days—to get rid of the sites. People were scared shitless that a nuclear war was coming, and soon a telecommunications hotline was set up between America and the U.S.S.R.. Just to be safe, the U.S., U.S.S.R., and a bunch of other nations signed on to a Nuclear Test Ban Treaty to further disarmament. Kennedy took a page from Eisenhower's book to deal with the smaller conflicts, and focused on a new policy of "flexible response" that discredited Dulles' one-size-fits-all shitshow of "massive retaliation."

TL;DR Kennedy messed up some shit in foreign policy, made us communicate a little better with the Soviets afterwards, and started ideas that he didn't get to finish cause he got shot in the head.

NOW, A JOHNSON

Kennedy is way more known than his Vice President, Lyndon B. Johnson, yet conversely, Johnson did way more to be known for. He was a 30 year Congress member, and was possibly the most productive man in the job. Inspired by his lowly roots and family in local politics, Johnson's plan was to make America a new "Great Society," in which the government eliminated poverty and let nobody go hungry. He expanded Kennedy's civil rights bill, passing the Civil Rights Act of 1964, which made it illegal to segregate any public facility, ratified the Twenty-Fourth Amendment, which made the poll tax (often used to keep poor African-Americans from voting) illegal, and passed a significant income tax cut, boosting economic growth in the sixties (but also government debt). Furthering his War on Poverty *("Never go to war with a noun" -Reif)*, Johnson created the Office of Economic Opportunity in 1964, which spend its billion dollar budget on a fuck ton of new programs, from preschool aid to legal services for the poor to vocational education. LBJ was re-elected in a landslide, and as Democrats basically controlled every branch of the government, he got a lot more shit done in the first half of his second term: Medicare, insurance for the old; Medicaid, insurance for the poor and disabled; the Elementary and Secondary Education Act, which helped out poor school districts; A new immigration law that abolished "quotas" for how many people could come from any one country per year; The National Foundation for the Arts and Humanities, which...funded the arts and humanities, duh; and he added to his cabinet a Department of Transportation and Department of Housing and Urban development. Even Johnson's wife got shit done, spending her tenure on a campaign for the environment called "Beautify America."

Along with the civil rights legislation passed earlier, Johnson's Voting Rights Act of 1965 ended literacy tests for voting, one of the South's last vestiges of legal discrimination. Changes like these made the South really fucking pissed, and in response local officials caused a bunch of little incidents, forcing the Federal Government to step in to keep things in order. MLK Jr. was leading peaceful Black resistance to the violent local officials; his 1963 March on Washington was one of the most successful demonstrations in history, with over 200,000 Whites and Blacks alike voicing support for the new civil rights bill. His March to Montgomery in 1965 was met with extreme police brutality, and LBJ was forced to send troops in to protect King and fellow demonstrators. On the more stubborn side of the resistance was Malcolm X, who claimed King was submitting to White oppression through his peaceful protests. After Malcolm X was assassinated 1965, other groups popped up in support of his ideas, like the separatist group the Black Panthers, led by Huey Newton and Bobby Seale. The Panthers were controversial force in the community, and were accused of starting a series of riots in the late sixties. Following these accusations, the civil rights movement took another major slap in the face when MLK was assassinated in April of 1968, and a fuck ton of riots broke out in over 100 cities the next day.

Other agendas grew across the country too, such as the Students for a Democratic Society, that supported a growing leftist movement. Starting at Berkeley in 1964, a bunch of students protested restrictions on free speech in universities everywhere, and soon enough this morphed into hating on other school rules, and somehow after that it became about protesting the Vietnam War. There was a violent version of the society called the "Weathermen," which was probably the least violent-sounding name possible. The countercultural agenda, which was basically to do nothing but drugs and sex, grew a LOT. Music from American artists like Bob Dylan and Janis Joplin blended with the Rock and Roll influences of the Beatles in Britain to create a generational soundtrack. Women used the momentum of defiance to push for greater acknowledgement, Betty Friedan founding the National Organization for Women (NOW) in 1966 and the whole lot campaigning for an equal rights amendment that would finally be passed in 1972. The Sexual revolution was underway as well, boosted by the 1965 case *Griswold v. Connecticut,* which ruled that no state could prohibit the use of contraceptives. *Yates v. United States* in 1957 and *Engel v. Vitale* in 1962 supported the countercultural growth as well, ruling respectively that radical speech (even from COMMIES) is legal and that states requiring religious education is not.

Speaking of Supreme court cases, it should be noted that Chief Justice Earl Warren made a major impact in the early sixties. In 1962, the case *Baker v. Carr* made major clarifications on how to keep voting fair, but even more impactful was Warren's oversight of four linked cases: *Mapp v. Ohio, Gideon v. Wainwright, Escobedo v. Illinois, and Miranda v. Arizona,* all of which would revolutionize the rights of a defendant in a court of law. This was really damned important too, because everyone in counterculture was challenging the law, just as everyone in the Civil Rights movement was.

TL;DR Lyndon B. Johnson did a shit ton of shit, but he wasn't the only one getting shit done. MLK and Malcolm X fought for Black rights, Betty Friedan and NOW fought for women's rights, and the Supreme Court of Earl Warren fought for and granted pretty much every right people were missing, from birth control to a defendant's rights in court.

VIETNAM: JOHNSON'S BIGGEST FUCK UP

When you're funneling all your cash into a gigantic war, you usually don't have much left over for founding a fuck ton of new social programs. Unfortunately for LBJ, he was passionate about spending a fuck ton of money on both causes, so his money-wasting failure in the Vietnam War is widely considered one of his—and one of America's—biggest fuck ups.

As conflict between the South and North Vietnamese nations built up in the early sixties, America had put a foot in the door and sent a few thousand troops to support the South. The Southern government was capitalist, but it also really sucked in terms of human rights, so even a lot of the South Vietnamese didn't support it. Just before Johnson became president, the leader of the South was assassinated and shit hit the fan. LBJ made things worse with the Tonkin Gulf Resolution, in which he used a false accusation of Vietnamese attacks on an American ship as an excuse to enter the war without Congress' permission.

Johnson sent hundreds of thousands of American troops to fight a losing battle, even using the draft for a military endeavor we didn't really have a place in. People got very pissed off by this move, watching U.S. involvement grow from light, supportable help under Ike to an illegal, forced war under Johnson. Things only got worse when the Northern Vietcong forces launched a really bloody surprise attack on American troops in 1968, and the "Tet offensive" took away so much of the already dwindling public support for the war that Johnson was forced to slow down. He even chose not to run again for president.

TL;DR Vietnam was a fucked up situation and we ended up fucking it up just a little more. Well, a lot more. So much more that Johnson didn't even campaign for a second term.

RICHARD NIXON FINALLY BECOMES PRESIDENT. IT DOESN'T LAST.

Let's bang out this section the same way Richard Nixon banged himself out of office (I would have saved the "banged out of office" pun for Clinton but I just thought of an even better one. Stay tuned).

Nixon, who consistently fucked things up, was coming off a pretty bad fuck up when he lost the Governorship of California in 1962. People thought he was done with politics, but he ran again anyway and got the Oval Office in 1968. Nixon just barely won the people's vote with his hawkish yet positive messages, but got a big electoral margin of victory. Why the big gap? Counter-culture was tiring as fuck. A lot of people were cool with just going back to "regular" culture, which at the time was conservative, and those voting in the electoral college got tired much easier than your average teenage voter who probably showed up to the polls on LSD.

Nixon, who became kind of a hermit in the Oval Office, was ironically focused on the rest of the world more so than domestic policy. The president and Henry Kissinger (his National Security Advisor turned Secretary of State), put together a plan that relieved tension with the soviets in the Cold War. Nixon also put together a so-so policy for dealing with Vietnam, called "Vietnamization," in which Nixon basically pulled a bunch of American troops out of the country, but gave Vietnam money to take the war over themselves (so we wouldn't be embarrassed to "give up" and lose). This set a precedent reflected in the *Nixon Doctrine*, which asserted that the United States might fund wars in Asia, but we would no longer be fighting in them. This kinda fell apart when Nixon sent a bunch of troops to Cambodia just because there were a lot of communist bases there. This hypocrisy didn't matter much, however, because in 1970, an even worse fuck up was brought to center stage when the public found out about the My Lai Massacre, in which a bunch of innocent, defenseless Vietnamese villagers were slaughtered by American troops in

1968. America really wasn't looking too good internationally. Elsewhere, Nixon visited communist China in 1972, which shocked people for sure, but at least kept us on good terms with Mao and his cronies. This relationship was used to create a better arms deal with the Soviets, resulting in the beginning of the SALT programs (Strategic Arms Limitation Talks).

At home, Nixon tried to slow down Johnson's programs by giving money and power back to state governments to figure out how to solve their own shit. This ended up starting fights with the Democratic Congress, and Nixon's efforts saw little success. Economically, "stagflation" occurred as money became devalued by inflation, but the policies trying to turn that inflation into economic growth were unsuccessful in showing any real progress. A little recession took place and wrapped up by around 1972. Nixon still got re-elected that year, but this term ended early when he had to resign due to the Watergate scandal. Basically, what happened with Watergate is your typical idea of a shitty spying plan. Nixon's "Committee to Re-Elect the President," which was literally fucking called CREEP, started doing creepy shit when they bugged the Democratic national HQ in 1972. By 1973, news of this was leaked and a bunch of shady ass conversations that Nixon had recorded between federal employees seemed to tie the president to the scandal. A messy, drawn out, ugly investigation led to his resignation (and the resignation of a bunch of other federal employees that were tired of Nixon's shit) on August 9th, 1974. As these investigations were going on, an oil crisis also happened when Israel was attacked by its neighbors and America defended it, causing those neighbors to stop selling us oil for a while.

TL;DR Nixon won semi-popularly in 1968, did a pretty sucky job with the economy, did a pretty good of job getting us out of Vietnam and keeping peace with the USSR, and then fucked it up by getting us more involved. He also broke a shit ton of laws (probably) by spying on his competitors and had to quit because of it.

GERALD FORD AND JIMMY CARTER: AMERICA'S OKAYEST PRESIDENTS

Gerald Ford, Nixon's ex-VP, was a pretty plain guy who became president by default after Nixon had to quit. He was no iconic figure, but you didn't have to be popular to be a lot more popular than Dick. His first move was pardoning Richard Nixon, which immediately

made him less popular, but it did kind of ease all the tension about the final days of Nixon's presidency, and gave Ford a clean slate to start his presidency on.

From 1974 to 1977, Ford investigated the CIA and dealt with the aftermath of Nixon's foreign policy choices. Remember Cambodia and the Nixon Doctrine? Well, both of those blew up in Ford's face: America was put to shame when Saigon, Vietnam fell to the enemy of the U.S. backed Vietnamese government, and Ford worked to help evacuate anxious Vietnamese survivors; and shit hit the fan in Cambodia when another group we supported fell to radical communists that killed over a million of their own, leading to a few American deaths as well. After these events, things settled down in Southeast Asia, contrary to Eisenhower's predicted "domino theory."

After Ford came Jimmy Carter, a Democrat who won partly because people were still pissed at Republicans and partly because the Republican he was running against was boring old Ford.

Carter, an informal, detail-driven guy, was a common man at heart, and ran the White House as such. He focused on supporting human rights, cutting off aid to countries in Latin America known for their violations of them, and even gradually gave the Panama Canal back to the Panamanians. Carter peaked right before a major shit storm with the Camp David Accords of 1978, in which he arranged a peace settlement between Egypt and Israel, by inviting the leaders of both nations to meet at the detached location of Camp David,

144

Maryland with Carter as their personal moderator. Following this success came the Iran hostage crisis, in which the U.S. embassy in Iran was taken over by Ayatollah Khomeini and his gang of Islamic fundamentalists, and the Americans inside were—duh—held hostage. Carter tried to rescue them in 1980 and fucked up, which would cause a loss of popularity he could never come back from, and give Ronald Reagan an idea for a major campaign promise.

Domestically, as the economy slowly struggled to find its footing, other, more social changes took place. Immigration rose drastically, sprouting not just from the usual places but now by refugees fleeing the countries we had fucked around in years before, like Vietnam and Cuba. Illegal immigrants entered the country in droves and this eventuated in the first laws to punish employers for hiring these undocumented immigrants. Minority groups everywhere pushed for more rights; following the Black liberation movements of the sixties came Hispanic, Native-American, and Asian movements of the seventies. The Gay Liberation movement took major steps as well, its leaders inspired by a riot protesting a shady police raid on the Stonewall Inn, a famous New York City gay bar.

TL;DR Ford was pretty boring and had to deal with some foreign policy shit Nixon left behind, Carter was a champion of the common man, until some common men turned into hostages, then he ended up fucking up and becoming unpopular.

REAGAN COULD LAUNCH FIREWORKS OFF YOUR ASS AND YOU'D TRY TO CATCH THEM MID-AIR AS A SOUVENIR

The first day of his presidency, shady alpha-male ex-actor ex-Democrat Ronald Reagan waltzed into the Oval Office and got all Carter's hostages released. The guy knew how to put on a performance.

After the wild, liberal seventies, Americans were ready to settle into a more conservative stride, and it started with

"Reaganomics." They called for lower taxes. Reagan provided. They called for less government spending on social programs. Reagan stopped providing (to the poor). They called for less business regulation. Reagan, once again, provided. When air traffic controllers went on strike, what did Ronald Reagan, A.K.A. the Great Communicator, do? He fired them. Talk about sending a goddamn message.

On the social side, Reagan was so popular that Republicans flooded the Congress just cause they had his face tied to the party name. Reagan also appointed Supreme Court Justices that held conservative views, including the first woman on the court, Sandra Day O'Connor, who worked with other appointees Antonin Scalia and Anthony Kelly to restrict abortions among other conservative issues. Reagan got re-elected in 1984 without blinking an eye.

His flaws? The guy loved America, for sure, but he had an even bigger hard on for his hatred of commies. Reagan basically launched "The Cold War 2" by hyping up patriotism, spending money to help anti-commies fight in Latin America. Despite his wife's, Nancy Reagan's, "Just Say No" Campaign, Ronald didn't really give a shit if the groups he was funding to fight were selling drugs to America. Reagan proved this when in 1986, he and colleague Oliver North secretly sold weapons to Iran so they could use the profits to fund the Nicaraguan contra...basically committing treason. Nothing stopped Reagan from his military shopping spree—not even the national debt. In his first term, it nearly doubled, a trend upwards that has been maintained through modern day America. The United States debt rose from billions to trillions in a matter of years to fund Reagan's projects; he even wanted to create a space-based system of anti-missile weapons that he called "the Strategic Defense Initiative" (and regular people called "Star Wars"). Reagan was popular because he always provided what people wanted, but ignored the fact that he sure as fuck couldn't afford any of it.

Despite a few foreign policy failures, like sending Americans into Lebanon in 1982 to support Israel, only to end up suffering heavy losses and a terrorist attack at the U.S. embassy, Reagan's strategy of "throw everything we have at the problem" did get some major results. Reagan and Soviet leader Mikhail Gorbachev got to talking (he was the great communicator after all), and the two worked together to stop the arms race before it got too expensive for everybody. The President even talked Gorbachev into helping him push Iran and Iraq to stop fighting, and therefore to clean up some of the mess he had made by selling Iran those American weapons just years before. Eventually, Reagan's administration closed at a high point when he got to real results in the falling of the Berlin Wall. He'd ushered in a new era of capitalism, and even though he did it by spending a shit ton of taxpayer money, he was still so popular that his Vice President George H.W. Bush was basically handed the 1988 election.

Bush's Job? Clean up all the fucking debt Reagan left everywhere. While breaking his impossible promise to keep taxes low made him suffer in popularity, his tactful clean up of the Cold War and skilled intervention into the new Iraq conflict (their dictator, Saddam Hussein, decided to march into Kuwait in the summer of 1990 and just start taking over oil fields) won him skyrocketing polls for the years to come. Bush had organized a coalition of U.N. forces (Diversity!), gathered about 500,000 American troops (Inclusion!), and actually asked the Congress for approval first (Nobody fucking does this anymore!) for Operation Desert Storm, which ended the conflict faster than you can say "Back to School Special!" At home, Bush's policy fizzled as he did little more than Reagan for the impoverished and uneducated. The next election went to Bill Clinton and the Democrats...and to be frank, it sucked dick.

TL;DR Ronald "I piss red, white, and blue" Reagan took office in 1980, fucked a bunch of shit up in the long run, but was so goddamn popular in the short run that the Republicans got 12 years of free presidency. His VP, George H.W. Bush, came next and cleaned up some of Reagan's mess. He didn't end up quite as popular, but overall the eighties were a major win for the Republicans.

THE ONE WITH EVERYTHING THAT HAPPENED FROM 1992 TO NOW

Seriously? Chill out kid, you won't need to know most of what happened past Carter to do well on any AP or SAT exam, and if you don't have a good general idea, watch some goddamn news. Jeez. Okay, okay, here's a hint. Look up "Monica Lewinsky," "The Dot Com Bubble," "Globalization," "Dubya," "NAFTA," and "9/11" and you will be MORE than set on American history. Monica Lewinsky's TED Talk was actually really good, so maybe check it out. Otherwise, you've probably lived through most of this shit, so just think back. Good luck with history. Thanks for reading our book. We worked really hard to "inspire" [trick] whoever you are to "grow your love for history" [give us your money].

TL;DR This section is like four words fuck you just read it. Bonus points if you got the reference in the title.

18425267R00084

Made in the USA
San Bernardino, CA
20 December 2018